The Archbishop's Ceiling

The setting is a room of a former Archbishop's palace in an East European capital – a room which is probably bugged by the secret police. The central character is a 50-year-old author, Sigmund, who, having embarrassed the current regime, is faced with the opportunity of defecting to the West. He is encouraged by two of his former friends, also writers – his compatriot Marcus, an ex-political prisoner now in favour with the regime, and Adrian, a visiting American with typically liberal ideals. The issue is complicated by Maya, poet and actress, who has been the mistress in turn of all three.

It is the complexity of the relationship of these four, the inextricable interweaving of politics, sex and art, and the constant uncertainty as to whether what anyone says can be overheard that make for a rich and deeply intriguing play which feeds both off post-Watergate paranoia and the residue of the Cold War.

First seen in America in 1977, *The Archbishop's Ceiling* has not yet been staged in Britain.

The front cover shows 'Drawing Hands', a lithograph by M.C. Escher (1948), © Copyright M.C. Escher Heirs, c/o J.W. Vermeulen, Prilly, Switzerland. The photograph of Arthur Miller on the back cover is by Inge Morath.

Arthur Miller

The Archbishop's Ceiling

With an Afterword by Christopher Bigsby

METHUEN · LONDON

First published in Great Britain in 1984 simultaneously in hardback and as a Methuen Paperback by Methuen London Ltd., 11 New Fetter Lane, London EC4P 4EE

British Library Cataloguing in Publication Data

Miller, Arthur
   The Archbishop's ceiling.–(Methuen modern
   plays)
   I. Title
   812'.52   PS3525.I5156

   ISBN 0-413-55870-3
   ISBN 0-413-55880-0 pbk

Printed in Great Britain by
Richard Clay (The Chaucer Press) Ltd,
Bungay, Suffolk

THE ARCHBISHOP'S CEILING

CAST

ADRIAN
MAYA
MARCUS
IRINA
SIGMUND

Act One

Some time ago.

The sitting-room in the former residence of the archbishop; a capital in Europe.

Judging by the depth of the casement around the window at Right, the walls must be two feet thick. The room has weight and power, its contents chaotic and sensuous. Decoration is early Baroque.

The ceiling is first seen: in high relief the Four Winds, cheeks swelling, and cherubims, darkened unevenly by soot and age.

Light is from a few lamps of every style, from a contemporary bridge lamp to something that looks like an electrified hookah, but the impression of a dark overcrowded room remains; the walls absorb light.

A grand piano, scarved; a large blue vase on the floor under it.

Unhung paintings, immense and dark, leaning against a wall, heavy gilt frames.

Objects of dull brass not recently polished.

Two or three long dark, carved chests topped with tasselled rose-coloured cushions.

A long vaguely decrepit brown leather couch with billowing cushions; a stately carved armchair, bolsters, oriental camel bags.

A pink velour settee, old picture magazines piled on its foot and underneath – Life, Stern, Europ-aeo . . .

A Bauhaus chair in chrome and black leather on one of the smallish Persian rugs.

A wide ornate rolltop desk, probably out of the Twenties, with a stuffed Falcon or gamebird on its top.

Contemporary books on shelves, local classics in leather.

A sinuous chaise in faded pink.

Layers of chaos.

At Up Right a doorway to the living quarters.

At Left a pair of heavy doors opening on a dimly lit corridor. More chests here, a few piled-up chairs. This corridor leads upstage into darkness (and the unseen stairway down to the front door.) The corridor wall is of large unfaced stones.

ADRIAN *is seated on a couch. He is relaxed, an attitude of waiting, legs crossed, arms spread wide. Now he glances up at the doorway to the living quarters, considers for a moment, then lifts up the couch cushions looking underneath. He stands and goes to a table lamp, tilts it over to look under its base. He looks about again, and peers into the open piano.*

He glances up at the doorway again, then examines the ceiling, his head turned straight up. With another glance at the doorway he proceeds to the window at Right and looks behind the drapes.

MAYA *enters from the living quarters with a coffee pot and two cups on a tray.*

ADRIAN. Tremendous view of the city from up here.

MAYA. Yes.

ADRIAN. Like seeing it from a plane. Or a dream.

He turns and approaches the couch, blows on his hands.

MAYA. Would you like one of his sweaters? I'm sorry there's no firewood.

ADRIAN. It's warm enough. He doesn't heat this whole house, does he?

MAYA. It's impossible – only this and the bedroom. But the rest of it's never used.

ADRIAN. I forgot how gloomy it is in here.

MAYA. It's a hard room to light. Wherever you put a lamp it makes the rest seem darker. I think there are too many unrelated objects – the eye can't rest here.

She laughs, offers a cup; he takes it.

ADRIAN. Thanks, Maya. (*Sitting.*) Am I interrupting something?

MAYA. I never do anything. When did you arrive?

ADRIAN. Yesterday morning. I was in Paris.

MAYA. And how long do you stay?

ADRIAN. Maybe tomorrow night – I'll see.

MAYA. So short!

ADRIAN. I had a sudden yen to come look around again – see some of the fellows. And you.

MAYA. They gave a visa so quickly?

ADRIAN. Took two days.

MAYA. How wonderful to be famous.

ADRIAN. I was surprised I got one at all – I've attacked them, you know.

MAYA. In the *New York Times*.

ADRIAN. Oh, you read it.

MAYA. Last fall, I believe.

ADRIAN. What'd you think of it?

MAYA. It was interesting. I partly don't remember. I was surprised you did journalism.

She sips. He waits; nothing more.

ADRIAN. I wonder if they care what anybody writes about them anymore.

MAYA. Yes, they do – very much, I think. But I really don't know. – How's your wife?

ADRIAN. Ruth? She's good.

MAYA. I liked her. She had a warm heart. I don't like many women.

ADRIAN. You look different.

MAYA. I'm two years older – and three kilos.

ADRIAN. It becomes you.

MAYA. Too fat.

ADRIAN. No . . . *zaftig*. You look creamy. You changed your hairdo.

MAYA. From *Vogue* magazine.

ADRIAN (*laughs*). That so! It's sporty.

MAYA. What brings you back?

ADRIAN. . . . Your speech is a thousand per cent better. More colloquial.

MAYA. I recite aloud from *Vogue* magazine.

ADRIAN. You're kidding.

MAYA. Seriously. Is all I read anymore.

ADRIAN. Oh go on with you.

MAYA. Everything in *Vogue* magazine is true.

ADRIAN. Like the girl in pantyhose leaning on her pink Rolls-Royce.

MAYA. Oh yes, is marvellous. One time there was a completely naked girl in a mink coat. (*She extends her foot.*) and one foot touching the bubble bath. Fantastic imagination.

It is the only modern art that really excites me.

ADRIAN (*laughs*).

MAYA. And their expressions, these girls. Absolutely nothing. Like the goddesses of the Greeks – beautiful, stupid, everlasting. This magazine is classical.

ADRIAN. You're not drinking anymore?

MAYA. Only after nine o'clock.

ADRIAN. Good. You seem more organised.

MAYA. Until nine o'clock.

They laugh. MAYA *sips. Slight pause.* ADRIAN *sips.*

ADRIAN. What's Marcus doing in London?

MAYA. His last novel is coming out there just now.

ADRIAN. That's nice. I hear it was a success here.

MAYA. Very much. – You say very much or . . . ?

ADRIAN. Very much so.

MAYA. Very much so. – What a language!

ADRIAN. You're doing great. You must practise a lot.

MAYA. Only when the English come to visit Marcus, or the Americans. – I have his number in London if you . . .

ADRIAN. I have nothing special to say to him.

Pause.

MAYA. You came back for one day?

ADRIAN. Well, three, really. I was in a symposium in the Sorbonne – about the contemporary novel – and it got so pompous I got a yen to sit down again with writers who had actual troubles. So I thought I'd stop by before I went home.

MAYA. You've seen anyone?

ADRIAN. Yes.

Slight pause.

MAYA (*he had reached for a pack of cigarettes; in the pause she turns to him quickly, to forgive his not elaborating*). . . . It's all right . . .

ADRIAN. I had dinner with Otto and Sigmund, and their

wives.

MAYA (*surprised*). Oh! – You should have called me.

ADRIAN. I tried three times.

MAYA. But Sigmund knows my number.

ADRIAN. You don't live here anymore?

MAYA. Only when Marcus is away. (*She indicates the bedroom doorway*.) He has that tremendous bathtub . . .

ADRIAN. I remember, yes. When'd you break up?

MAYA. I don't remember – eight or nine months, I think. We are friends. Sigmund didn't tell you?

ADRIAN. Nothing. Maybe 'cause his wife was there.

MAYA. Why? I am friends with Elizabeth. So you have a new novel, I suppose.

ADRIAN (*laughs*). You make it sound like I have one every week.

MAYA. I always think you write so easily.

ADRIAN. I always have. But I just abandoned one that I worked on for two years. I'm still trying to get up off the floor. I forgot how easy you are to talk to.

MAYA. But you seem nervous.

ADRIAN. Just sexual tension.

MAYA. You wanted to make love tonight?

ADRIAN. If it came to it, sure. (*He takes her hand.*) In Paris we were in the middle of a discussion of Marxism and surrealism and I suddenly got this blinding vision of the inside of your thigh . . .

She laughs, immensely pleased.

. . . so I'm here.

He leans over and kisses her on the lips. Then he stands.

Incidentally . . . Ruth and I never married, you know.

MAYA (*surprised*). But didn't you call each other . . . ?

ADRIAN. We never did, really, but we never bothered to correct people. It just made it easier to travel and live together.

MAYA. And now?

ADRIAN. We're apart together. I want my own fireplace, but with a valid plane ticket on the mantel.

MAYA. Well that's natural, you're a man.

ADRIAN. In my country I'm a child and a son of a bitch. But I'm toying with the idea of growing up – I may ask her to marry me.

MAYA. Is that necessary?

ADRIAN. You're a smart girl – that's exactly the question.

MAYA. Whether it was necessary.

ADRIAN. Not exactly that – few books are necessary; a writer has to write. It's that it became absurd, suddenly – here I'm laying out motives, characterisations, secret impulses – the whole psychological chess game – when the truth is I'm not sure anymore that I believe in psychology. That anything we think really determines what we're going to do. Or even what we feel. This interest you?

MAYA. You mean anyone can do anything.

ADRIAN. Almost. Damn near. But the point is a little different. Ruth – when we came back from here two years ago – she went into a terrible depression. She'd had them before, but this time she seemed suicidal.

MAYA. Oh my God. Why?

ADRIAN. Who knows? There were so many reasons there was no reason. She went back to psychiatry. Other therapies . . . nothing worked. Finally, they gave her a pill.

Slight pause.

It was miraculous. Turned her completely around. She's full of energy, purpose, optimism. Looks five years younger.

MAYA. A chemical.

ADRIAN. Yes. She didn't have the psychic energy to pull her stockings up. Now they've just made her assistant to the managing editor of her magazine. Does fifty laps a day in the swimming pool – It plugged her in to some . . . some power. And she lit up.

MAYA. She is happy?

ADRIAN. I don't really know – she doesn't talk about her mind anymore, her soul; she talks about what she does. Which is terrific . . .

MAYA. But boring.

ADRIAN. In a way, maybe – but you can't knock it; I really think it saved her life. But what bothers me is something else.

Slight pause.

She knows neither more nor less about herself now than when she was trying to die. The interior landscape has not changed. What has changed is her reaction to power. Before she feared it, now she enjoys it. Before she fled from it, now she seeks it. She got plugged in, and she's come alive.

MAYA. So you have a problem.

ADRIAN. What problem do you think I have?

MAYA. It is unnecessary to write novels anymore.

ADRIAN. God, you're smart – yes. It made me think of Hamlet. Here we are tracking that marvellous maze of his mind, but isn't that slightly ludicrous when one knows that with the right pill his anxiety would dissolve? Christ, he's got everything to live for, heir to the throne, servants, horses – correctly medicated he could have made a deal with the king and married Ophelia. Or Socrates – instead of hemlock, a swig of Lithium and he'd end up the mayor of Athens and live to a hundred. What is lost? Some wisdom, some knowledge found in suffering. But knowledge is power, that's why it's good – so what is wrong with gaining power without having to suffer at all?

MAYA (*with the faintest colour of embarrassment, it seems*). You have some reason to ask me this question?

ADRIAN. Yes.

MAYA. Why?

ADRIAN. You have no pills in this country, but power is very sharply defined here. The government makes it very clear that you must snuggle up to power or you will never be happy.

Slight pause.

I'm wondering what that does to people, Maya. Does it smooth them all out when they know they must all plug-in or their lights go out regardless of what they think, or their personalities?

MAYA. I have never thought of this question. (*She glances at her watch.*) I am having a brandy, will you? (*She stands.*)

ADRIAN (*laughs*). It's nine o'clock?

MAYA. In one minute.

She goes upstage, pours.

ADRIAN. I'd love one; thanks.

MAYA. But I have another mystery.

She carefully pours two glasses. He waits. She brings him one, remains standing.

Cheers.

ADRIAN. Cheers.

They drink.

Wow – that's good.

MAYA. I prefer whisky, but he locks it up when he is away.

She sits apart from him.

I have known intimately so many writers; they all write books condemning people who wish to be successful, and praised, who desire some power in life. But I have never met one writer who did not wish to be praised, and successful . . . (*She is smiling.*) . . . and even powerful. Why do they condemn others who wish the same for themselves?

ADRIAN. Because they understand them so well.

MAYA. For this reason I love *Vogue* magazine.

He laughs.

I am serious. In this magazine everyone is successful. No one has ever apologised because she was beautiful and happy. I believe this magazine.

She knocks back the remains of her drink, stands, goes towards the liquor upstage.

Tell me the truth – why have you come back?

ADRIAN (*slight pause*). You think I could write a book about this country?

She brings down the bottle, fills his glass.

MAYA. No, Adrian.

ADRIAN. I'm too American.

MAYA. No, the Russians cannot either.

She refills her own glass.

A big country cannot understand small possibilities. When it is raining in Moscow, the sun is shining in Tashkent. Terrible snow in New York, but it is a beautiful day in Arizona. In a small country, when it rains it rains everywhere.

She sits beside him.

Why have you come back?

ADRIAN. I've told you.

MAYA. Such a trip – for three days?

ADRIAN. Why not? I'm rich.

MAYA (*she examines his face*). You are writing a book about us.

ADRIAN. I've written it, and abandoned it. I want to write it again.

MAYA. About this country.

ADRIAN. About you.

MAYA. But what do you know about me?

ADRIAN. Practically nothing. But something in me knows

everything.

MAYA. I am astonished.

ADRIAN. My visa's good through the week – I'll stay if we could spend a lot of time together. Could we? It'd mean a lot to me.

An instant. She get up, goes to a drawer and takes out a new pack of cigarettes.

I promise nobody'll recognise you – the character is blonde and very tall and has a flat chest. What do you say?

MAYA. But why?

ADRIAN. I've become obsessed with this place, it's like some Jerusalem for me.

MAYA. But we are of no consequence . . .

ADRIAN. Neither is Jerusalem, but it always has to be saved. Let me stay here with you till Friday. When is Marcus coming back?

MAYA. I never know – not till spring, probably. Is he also in your book?

ADRIAN. In a way. Don't be mad, I swear you won't be recognised.

MAYA. You want me to talk about him?

ADRIAN. I'd like to understand him, that's all.

MAYA. For example?

ADRIAN. Well . . . let's see. You know, I've run into Marcus in three or four countries the past five years; had long talks together, but when I go over them in my mind I realise he's never said anything at all about himself. I like him, always glad to see him, but he's a total blank. For instance, how does he manage to get a house like this?

MAYA. But why not?

ADRIAN. It belongs to the government, doesn't it?

MAYA. It is the same way he gets everything – his trips abroad, his English suits, his girls . . .

ADRIAN. How?

MAYA. He assumes he deserves them.

ADRIAN. But his money – he seems to have quite a lot.

MAYA (*shrugs, underplaying the fact*). He sells his father's books from time to time. He had a medieval collection . . .

ADRIAN. They never confiscate such things?

MAYA. Perhaps they haven't thought of it. You are the only person I know who thinks everything in a Socialist country is rational.

ADRIAN. In other words, Marcus is a bit of an operator.

MAYA. Marcus? Marcus is above all naive.

ADRIAN. Naive! You don't mean that.

MAYA. No one but a naive man spends six years in prison, Adrian.

ADRIAN. But in that period they were arresting everybody, weren't they?

MAYA. By no means everybody. Marcus is rather a brave man.

ADRIAN. Huh! I had him all wrong. What do you say, let me bring my bag over.

MAYA. You have your book with you?

ADRIAN. No, it's home.

She seems sceptical.

. . . Why would I carry it with me?

She stares at him with the faintest smile.

What's happening?

MAYA. I don't know – what do you think?

She gets up and cradling her glass walks thoughtfully to another seat and sits. He gets up and comes to her.

ADRIAN. What is it?

She shakes her head. She seems overwhelmed by some wider sadness. His tone now is uncertain.

Maya?

MAYA. You've been talking to Allison Wolfe?

ADRIAN. I've talked to him, yes.

She stands, moves, comes to a halt.

MAYA. He is still telling that story?

ADRIAN (*slight pause*). I didn't believe him, Maya.

MAYA. He's a vile gossip.

ADRIAN. He's a writer, all writers are gossips.

MAYA. He is a vile man.

ADRIAN. I didn't believe him.

MAYA. What did he say to you?

ADRIAN. Why go into it?

MAYA. I want to know. Please.

ADRIAN. It was ridiculous, I know that. Allison has a puritan
imagination.

MAYA. Tell me what he said.

ADRIAN (*slight pause*). Well . . . that you and Marcus . . .
look, it's so stupid . . .

MAYA. That we have orgies here?

ADRIAN. . . . . Yes.

MAYA. And we bring in young girls?

He is silent.

Adrian?

ADRIAN. That this house is bugged. And you bring in girls
to compromise writers with the government.

Pause.

MAYA. You'd better go, I believe.

He is silent for a moment, observing her. She is full.

I'm tired anyway . . . I was just going to bed when you
called.

ADRIAN. Maya, if I believed it, would I have talked as I have
in here?

MAYA (*smiling*). I don't know, Adrian – would you? Anyway,
you have your passport. Why not?

ADRIAN. You know I understand the situation too well to believe Allison. Resistance is impossible anymore. I know

the government's got the intellectuals in its pocket, and the few who aren't have stomach ulcers.

He comes to her, takes her hand.

I *was* nervous when I came in but it was sexual tension – I knew we'd be alone.

Her suspicion remains; she slips her hand out of his.

. . . All right, I did think of it. But that's inevitable, isn't it?

MAYA. Yes, of course.

She moves away again.

ADRIAN. It's hard for anyone to know what to believe in this country, you can understand that.

MAYA. Yes.

She sits, lonely.

ADRIAN (*sits beside her*). Forgive me, will you?

MAYA. It is terrible.

ADRIAN. What do you say we forget it?

She looks at him with uncertainty.

What are you doing now?

MAYA (*slight pause. She stares front for a moment, then taking a breath as though resolving to carry on, her tone brightens*).

I write for the radio.

ADRIAN. No plays anymore?

MAYA. I can't work that hard anymore.

ADRIAN. They wouldn't put them on?

MAYA. Oh, they would – I was never political, Adrian.

ADRIAN. You were, my first time . . .

MAYA. Well everybody was in those days. But it wasn't really politics.

ADRIAN. What then?

MAYA. I don't know – some sort of illusion that we could be Communists without having enemies. It was a childishness, dancing around the Maypole. It could never last, life is not like that.

ADRIAN. What do you write?

MAYA. I broadcast little anecdotes; amusing things I notice on the streets, the trams. I am on once a week; they have me on Saturday mornings for breakfast. What is it you want to know?

ADRIAN. I'm not interviewing you, Maya.

MAYA (*she stands suddenly, between anger and fear*). Why have you come?

ADRIAN (*stands*). I've told you, Maya – I thought maybe I could grab hold of the feeling again.

MAYA. Of what?

ADRIAN. This country, this situation. It escapes me the minute I cross the border. It's like some goddamned demon that only lives here.

MAYA. But we are only people, what is so strange?

ADRIAN. I'll give you an example – it's an hour from Paris here; we sit down to dinner last night in a restaurant and two plainclothesmen take the next table. It was blatant. Not the slightest attempt to disguise that they were there to intimidate Sigmund and Otto. They kept staring straight at them.

MAYA. But why did he take you to a restaurant? Elizabeth could have given you dinner.

ADRIAN. . . . I don't understand.

MAYA. But Sigmund knows that will happen if he walks about with a famous American writer.

ADRIAN. You're not justifying it . . . ?

MAYA. I have not been appointed to justify or condemn anything. (*She laughs.*) And neither has Sigmund. He is an artist, a very great writer, and that is what he should be doing.

ADRIAN. I can't believe what I'm hearing, Maya.

MAYA (*laughs*). But you must, Adrian. You really must believe it.

ADRIAN. You mean it's perfectly all right for two cops to be
. . .

MAYA. But that is their *business*. But it is not Sigmund's business to be taunting the government. Do you go about trying to infuriate your CIA, your FBI?
He is silent.
Of course not. You stay home and write your books. Just
as the Russian writers stay home and write theirs . . .

ADRIAN. But Sigmund isn't permitted to write his books .
. .

MAYA. My God – don't you understand *anything*?
*The sudden force of her outburst is mystifying to him. He looks
at her, perplexed. She gathers herself.*
I'm very tired, Adrian. Perhaps we can meet again before
you leave.

ADRIAN. Okay. (*He looks about.*) I forgot where I put my
coat . . .

MAYA. I hung it inside.
She goes upstage and out through the doorway. ADRIAN, *his
face taut, looks around at the room, up at the ceiling. She returns, hands him the coat.*
You know your way back to the hotel?

ADRIAN. I'll find it.
He extends his hand, she takes it.
I'm not as simple as I seem, Maya.

MAYA. I'm sorry I got excited.

ADRIAN. I understand – you don't want him taking risks.

MAYA. Why should he? Especially when things are improv-
ing all the time anyway.

ADRIAN. They aren't arresting anybody . . .

MAYA. Of course not. Sigmund just can't get himself to
admit it so he does these stupid things. One can live as
peacefully as anywhere.

ADRIAN (*putting on his coat*). Still, it's not every country that writers keep a novel manuscript behind their fireplace.

MAYA (*stiffening*). Goodnight.

ADRIAN (*he sees her cooled look . . . slight pause*). Goodnight, Maya.

He crosses the room to the double doors at Left, and as he opens one . . .

MAYA. Adrian?

He turns in the doorway.

You didn't really mean that, I hope.

He is silent. She turns to him.

No one keeps manuscripts behind a fireplace anymore. You know that.

ADRIAN (*looks at her for a moment, and with irony*). . . . Right.

He stands there, hand on the doorhandle, looking down at the floor, considering. He smiles, turning back to her.

Funny how life imitates art; the melodrama kept flattening out my characterisations. It's an interesting problem – whether it matters who anyone is or what anyone thinks, when all that counts anymore – is power.

He goes brusquely into the corridor, walks upstage into darkness. She hesitates then rushes out, closing the door behind her, and calls up the corridor.

MAYA (*a suppressed call*). Adrian? (*She waits.*) Adrian!

He reappears from the darkness and stands shaking his head, angry and appalled. She has stiffened herself against her confession.

We can talk out here, it is only in the apartment.

ADRIAN. Jesus Christ, Maya.

MAYA. I want you to come inside for a moment – you should not have mentioned Sigmund's manuscript . . .

ADRIAN (*stunned, a look of disgust – adopting her muffled tone*). Maya . . . how can you do this?

MAYA (*with an indignant note*). They never knew he has written a novel, how dare you mention it! Did he give it to you?

ADRIAN. My head is spinning, what the hell is this . . . ?

MAYA. Did he give it to you?

ADRIAN (*a flare of open anger*). How can I tell you anything
. . . ?

MAYA. Come inside. Say that you have sent it to Paris. Come
. . .

She starts for the door.

ADRIAN. How the hell would I send it to Paris?

MAYA. They'll be searching his house now, they'll destroy it!
You must say that you sent it today with some friend of
yours.

She pulls him by the sleeve.

ADRIAN (*freeing himself*). Wait a minute – you mean they
were taping us in bed?

MAYA. I don't know. I don't know when it was installed.
Please . . . simply say that you have sent the manuscript
to Paris. Come.

She grasps the door handle.

ADRIAN (*stepping back from the door*). That's a crime.

She turns to him with a contemptuous look.

Well it is, isn't it? Anyway, I didn't say it was his book.

MAYA. It was obviously him. Say you have sent it out! You
must!

*She opens the door instantly, enters the room, and speaking in
a relaxed, normal tone . . .*

Perhaps you'd better stay until the rain lets up. I might
go to bed, but why don't you make yourself comfortable?

ADRIAN (*he hesitates in the corridor, then enters the room. He
stands there in silence, glancing about*). . . . All right.
Thanks.

He stands there silent, in his fear.

MAYA. Yes?

ADRIAN. Incidentally.

He breaks off. A long hiatus. He is internally positioning himself to the situation.

. . . that manuscript I mentioned.

MAYA. Yes?

ADRIAN. It's in Paris by now. I . . . gave it to a friend who was leaving this morning.

MAYA. Oh?

ADRIAN. Yes.

Slight pause. It occurs to him suddenly . . .

A girl.

MAYA (*as though amused*). You already have girls here?

ADRIAN (*starting to grin*). Well not really – she's a cousin of mine. Actually, a second cousin. Just happened to meet her on the street. All right if I have another brandy?

MAYA. Of course.

He pours.

ADRIAN. I'll be going in a minute.

He sits in his coat on the edge of a chair with his glass.

Just let me digest this. This drink, I mean.

She sits on the edge of another chair a distance away.

Quite an atmosphere in this house. I never realised it before.

MAYA. It's so old. Sixteenth century, I think.

ADRIAN. It's so alive – once you're aware of it.

MAYA. They built very well in those days.

ADRIAN (*directly to her*). Incredible. I really didn't believe it.

MAYA. Please go.

ADRIAN. In one minute. Did I dream it or did it belong to the archbishop?

MAYA. It was his residence.

ADRIAN (*looks up to the ceiling*). That explains the cherubims . . . (*He looks at his drink.*) . . . and the antonyms.

She stands.

I'm going. This is . . . (*He looks around.*) . . . this is what

I never got into my book – this doubleness. This density with angels hovering overhead. Like power always with you in a room. Like God, in a way. Just tell me – do you ever get where you've forgotten it?

MAYA. I don't really live here anymore.

ADRIAN. Why? You found this style oppressive?

MAYA. I don't hear the rain. Please.

ADRIAN (*stands facing her*). I'm not sure I should but I'm filling up with sympathy. I'm sorry as hell, Maya.
She is silent.
I could hire a car – let's meet for lunch and take a drive in the country.

MAYA. All right. I'll pick you up at the hotel. (*She starts past him toward the doors.*)

ADRIAN (*he takes her hand as she passes*). Thirty seconds. Please. I want to chat. Just to hear myself. (*Moving her to a chair.*) Half a minute . . . just in case you don't show up.

MAYA (*sitting*). Of course I will.

ADRIAN (*clings to her hand, kneebends before her*). I've never asked you before – you ever been married?
She laughs.

ADRIAN. Come on, give me a chat. Were you?

MAYA. Never, no.

ADRIAN. And what were your people – middle class?

MAYA. Workers. They died of flu in the war.

ADRIAN. Who brought you up?

MAYA. The nuns.

ADRIAN (*stands; looks around*). . . . . Is it always like a performance? Like we're quoting ourselves?

MAYA (*she stands*). Goodnight.
She goes and opens a door.

ADRIAN. My God – you poor girl.
He takes her into his arms and kisses her.
Maybe I should say – in all fairness – (*Leaving her, he ad-*

dresses the ceiling.) that the city looks much cleaner than
my last time. And there's much more stuff in the shops.
And the girls have shaved their legs. In fact – (*He turns to
her – she is smiling.*) this is the truth – I met my dentist in
the hotel this morning. He's crazy about this country!
(*With a wild underlay of laughter.*) Can't get over the way
he can walk the streets any hour of the night, which is impossible in New York. Said he'd never felt so relaxed and
free in his whole life! And at that very instant, Sigmund
and Otto walked into the lobby and he congratulated them
on having such a fine up-and-coming little civilisation!
He suddenly yells at the top of his lungs.

Forgive me, I scream in New York, sometimes.

*She is half-smiling, alert to him; he comes to the open doorway
and grasps her hands.*

Goodnight. And if I never see you again . . .

MAYA. I'll be there, why not?

ADRIAN. How do I know? But just in case – I want you to
know that I'll never forget you in that real short skirt you
wore last time, and the moment when you slung one leg
over the arm of the chair. You have a sublime sluttishness,
Maya – don't be mad, it's a gift when it's sublime.

She laughs.

How marvellous to see you laugh – come, walk me downstairs.

He pulls her through the doorway.

MAYA. It's too cold out here . . .

ADRIAN (*shuts the door to the room, draws her away from it*).
For old times' sake . . .

MAYA. We'll talk tomorrow.

ADRIAN (*with a wild smile, excited eyes*). You're a government agent?

MAYA. What can I say? Will you believe anything?

ADRIAN (*on the verge of laughter*). My spine is tingling. In my

book, Maya – I may as well tell you, I've been struggling
with my sanity the last ten minutes – in my book I made
you an agent who screws all the writers and blackmails
them so they'll give up fighting the government. And I
abandoned it because I finally decided it was too melodramatic, the characters got lost in the plot. I invented it
and I didn't believe it; and I'm standing here looking at
you and *I still don't believe it*!

MAYA. Why should you?

ADRIAN (*instantly, pointing into her face*). That's what you say
in the book! (*He grasps her hand passionately in both of his.*)
Maya, listen – you've got to help me. I believe in your
goodness. I don't care what you've done, I still believe that
deep inside you're a rebel and you hate this goddamned
government. You've got to tell me – I'll stay through the
week – we'll talk, and you're going to tell me what goes
on in your body, in your head in this situation.

MAYA. . . . Wait a minute . . .

ADRIAN (*kissing her hands*). Maya, you've made me believe
in my book!

*She suddenly turns her head. He does. Then he sees her ap-
prehension.*

ADRIAN. You expecting somebody?

Voices are heard now from below. She is listening.

Maya?

MAYA (*mystified*). Perhaps some friends of Marcus.

ADRIAN. He gives out the key?

MAYA. Go, please. Goodnight.

She enters the room. He follows her in.

ADRIAN. You need any help?

*A MAN and WOMAN appear from upstage darkness in the cor-
ridor.*

MAYA. No – no, I am not afraid . . . (*She moves him to the
door.*)

ADRIAN. I'll be glad to stay . . .

He turns, sees the man, who is just approaching the door, a valise in his hand, wearing a raincoat.

For Christ's sake – it's Marcus!

MARCUS *is older, fifty-eight. He puts down his valise, spreads out his arms.*

MARCUS. Adrian!

Laughter. A GIRL, *beautiful, very young, stands a step behind him as he and* ADRIAN *embrace.*

MAYA (*within the room*). Marcus?

MARCUS (*entering the room*). You're here, Maya! This is marvellous.

He gives her a peck. The GIRL *enters, stands there looking around.*

(*To* ADRIAN.) A friend of yours is parking my car, he'll be delighted to see you.

ADRIAN. Friend of *mine?*

MARCUS. Sigmund.

MAYA. Sigmund?

ADRIAN. Sigmund's *here?*

MARCUS. He's coming up for a drink. We ran into each other at the airport. (*To* MAYA.) Is there food? (*to* ADRIAN.) You'll stay, won't you? I'll call some people, we can have a party.

ADRIAN. Party? (*Flustered, glances at* MAYA.) Well . . . yeah, great!

An understanding outburst of laughter between him and MARCUS.

MAYA. There's only some ham. I'm going home.

She turns to go upstage to the bedroom.

MARCUS (*instantly*). Oh no, Maya! – You mustn't. I was going to call you first thing . . . (*Recalling.*) Wait, I have something for you.

He hurriedly zips open a pocket of his valise, takes out a pair of shoes in tissue.

I had an hour in Frankfurt. Look, dear . . .

He unwraps the tissue. Her face lights. She half unwillingly takes them.

MAYA. Oh my God.

MARCUS *laughs. She kicks off a shoe and tries one on.*

MARCUS. Right size?

IRINA (*as* MAYA *puts on the other shoe*). Highly beautiful.

MAYA *takes a few steps watching her feet, then goes to* MARCUS *and gives him a kiss, then looks into his eyes with a faint smile, her longing and hatred.*

MARCUS (*taking out folds of money*). Here, darling . . . ask Mrs Andrus to prepare something, will you? (*Handing her money.*) Let's have an evening. (*He starts her toward the bedroom door upstage.*) But come and put something on, it's raining. (*And comes face to face with the* GIRL.) Oh, excuse me – this is Irina . . .

MAYA *barely nods, and goes back to pick up her other shoes.*

ADRIAN. I'll go along with you, Maya – (*He reaches for his coat.*)

MARCUS. No, it's only down the street. Irina, this is my good friend, Maya.

IRINA. 'Aloo.

MAYA *silently shakes her hand.*

MARCUS. And here is Adrian Wallach. Very important American writer.

MAYA *exits upstage.*

ADRIAN. How do you do?

IRINA. 'Aloo. I see you Danemark.

ADRIAN. She's going to see me in Denmark?

MARCUS. She's Danish. But she speaks a little English.

IRINA (*with forefinger and thumb barely separated – to* ADRIAN).

Very small.

ADRIAN. When do you want to meet in Denmark?

MAYA enters putting on a raincoat.

MAYA. Sausages?

MARCUS. And maybe some cheese and bread and some fruit. I'll open wine.

IRINA. I see your book.

ADRIAN (*suddenly – as* MAYA *goes for the door*). Wait! – I'll walk her there . . .

MAYA hesitates at the door.

MARCUS (*grasping* ADRIAN's *arm, laughing*). No-no-no, you are our guest; please, it's only two doors down. Maya doesn't mind.

MAYA starts out to the door. SIGMUND *appears in the corridor. A heavy man shaking out his raincoat. He is in his late forties. She halts before the doorway.*

MAYA (*questioningly; but with a unique respect*). Sigmund.

SIGMUND. Maya.

He kisses the palm of her hand. For a moment they stand facing each other.

MARCUS. Look who we have here, Sigmund!

MAYA exits up the corridor as SIGMUND *enters the room.*

SIGMUND. Oh – my friend!

He embraces ADRIAN, *laughing, patting his back.*

ADRIAN. How's it going, Sigmund? (*Grasping* SIGMUND's *hand.*) What a terrific surprise! How's your cold, did you take my pills?

SIGMUND. Yes, thank you. I take pills, vodka, brandy, whisky – now I have only headache. (*With a nod to* IRINA.) Grüss Gött.

MARCUS goes and opens a chest, brings bottles and glasses to the marble table.

IRINA. *Grüss Gött.*

ADRIAN. Oh, you speak German?

IRINA (*with the gesture*). Very small.

MARCUS. Come, help yourselves. (*Taking a key ring out of his valise.*) I have whisky for you, Adrian.

ADRIAN. I'll drink brandy, how about you, Sigmund?

SIGMUND. For me whisky.

MARCUS (*taking out an address book*). I'll call a couple of people, all right?

ADRIAN. *Girls!*

SIGMUND *sits downstage, takes out a cigarette.*

MARCUS. If you feel like it.

ADRIAN (*glancing at* SIGMUND *who is lighting up*). Maybe better just us.

MARCUS. Sigmund likes a group. (*He picks up his valise.*)

SIGMUND. What you like.

ADRIAN. (*To* MARCUS). Well okay.

MARCUS (*pointing upstage to* IRINA). Loo?

IRINA. Oh ya!

He holds her by the waist carrying the valise in his free hand, as they move upstage he says to SIGMUND.) We can talk in the bedroom in a little while.

He exits with IRINA.

ADRIAN. That's a nice piece of Danish.

SIGMUND *draws on his cigarette.* ADRIAN *gets beside him and taps his shoulder;* SIGMUND *turns up to him.* ADRIAN *points to ceiling, then to his own ear.*

Capish?

SIGMUND *turns front, expressionless.*

SIGMUND. The police have confiscated my manuscript.

ADRIAN (*his hand flies out to grip* SIGMUND'*s shoulder*). No! Oh Jesus – when?

SIGMUND. Now. Tonight.

ADRIAN (*glancing quickly around*). He had a record player . . .

SIGMUND (*a contemptuous wave toward the ceiling*). No – I don't care.

ADRIAN. The last fifteen-twenty minutes you mean?

SIGMUND. Tonight. They have take it away.

ADRIAN. My God, Sigmund . . .

SIGMUND turns to him.

I mentioned something to Maya, but I had no idea it was really . . .

Breaks off, pointing to the ceiling.

SIGMUND. When, you told Maya?

ADRIAN. In the last fifteen minutes or so.

SIGMUND. No – they came earlier – around six o'clock.

ADRIAN. Nearly stopped my heart . . .

SIGMUND. No, I believe they find out for different reason.

ADRIAN. Why?

SIGMUND. I was so happy. (*Pause.*)

ADRIAN. So they figured you'd finished the book?

SIGMUND. I think so. I worked five years on this novel.

ADRIAN. How would they know you were happy?

SIGMUND (*pause. With a certain projection*). In this city, a man my age who is happy, attract attention.

ADRIAN. . . . . Listen. When I leave tomorrow you can give . . .

He stops himself, glances upstage to the bedroom doorway, taking out a notebook and pencil. As he writes . . . speaking in a tone of forced relaxation . . .

Before I leave you've got to give me a tour of the Old Roman bath . . .

He shows the page to SIGMUND who reads it and looks up at him.

SIGMUND *shakes his head negatively.*

ADRIAN (*horrified*). They've got the only . . . ?

SIGMUND *nods positively and turns away.*

ADRIAN (*appalled*). Sigmund – why?

SIGMUND. I thought would be safer with . . . (*He holds up a single finger.*)

Pause. ADRIAN *keeps shaking his head.*

ADRIAN (*sotto*). What are you doing here?

SIGMUND. I met him in the airport by accident.

ADRIAN. What were you doing at the airport?

SIGMUND. To tell my wife. She works there.

ADRIAN. I thought she was a chemist.

SIGMUND. She is wife to me – they don't permit her to be chemist. She clean the floor, the windows in the airport.

ADRIAN. Oh my God, Sigmund . . . (*Pause.*) Is there anything you can do?

SIGMUND. I try.

ADRIAN. Try what?

SIGMUND *thumbs upstage.*

Could he?

SIGMUND *throws up his chin – tremendous influence.*

Would he?

SIGMUND *holding a telephone to his mouth, then indicates the bedroom doorway.*

Really? To help?

SIGMUND. Is possible.

ADRIAN. Can you figure him out?

SIGMUND *extends a hand and rocks it, an expression of uncertainty on his face.*

ADRIAN. And Maya?

SIGMUND (*for a moment he makes no answer*). Woman is always complicated.

ADRIAN. You know that they . . . lie a lot.

SIGMUND. Yes.

Slight pause. He looks now directly into ADRIAN's *eyes.*

Sometimes not.

ADRIAN. You don't think it's time to seriously consider . . . (*He spreads his arms wide like a plane, lifting them forward in a take-off – then points in a gesture of flight.*) What I mentioned at dinner?

SIGMUND *emphatically nods 'No', while pointing downward – he'll remain here.*

ADRIAN. When we leave here I'd like to discuss whether there's really any point in that anymore.

SIGMUND *turns to him.*

I don't know if it was in your papers, but there's a hearing problem all over the world. Especially among the young. Rock music, traffic – modern life is too loud for the human ear – you understand me. The subtler sounds don't get through much anymore.

SIGMUND *faces front, expressionless.*

On top of that there's a widespread tendency in New York, Paris, London, for people to concentrate almost exclusively on shopping.

SIGMUND. I have no illusion.

ADRIAN. I hope not – shopping and entertainment. Sigmund?

SIGMUND *turns to him, and he points into his face, then makes a wide gesture to take in the room, the situation.*

Not entertaining. Not on anybody's mind in those cities.

SIGMUND. I know.

ADRIAN. Boring.

SIGMUND. Yes.

ADRIAN. Same old thing. It's the wrong style.

SIGMUND. I know.

ADRIAN. I meant what I said last night; I'd be happy to support – (*He points at* SIGMUND *who glances at him.*) until a connection is made with a university. (*He points to himself.*) Guarantee that.

SIGMUND *nods negatively and spreads both hands – he will stay here.*

We can talk about it later. I'm going to ask you why. I don't understand the point anymore. Not after this.

SIGMUND. You would also if it was your country.

ADRIAN. I doubt it. I would protect my talent. I saw a movie once where they bricked up a man in a wall.

MARCUS *enters in a robe, opening a whisky bottle.*

MARCUS. A few friends may turn up. (*He sets the whisky bottle on the marble table. To* ADRIAN.) Will you excuse us for a few minutes? Sigmund? (*He indicates the bedroom.*)

SIGMUND. I have told him.

MARCUS *turns to* ADRIAN *with a certain embarrassment.*

ADRIAN. They wouldn't destroy it, would they?

MARCUS *seems suddenly put-upon, and unable to answer.* Do you know?

MARCUS (*with a gesture toward the bedroom; to* SIGMUND). Shall we?

SIGMUND (*standing*). I would like Adrian to hear.

ADRIAN (*to* MARCUS). Unless you don't feel . . .

MARCUS (*unwillingly*). No – if he wishes, I have no objection. SIGMUND *sits.*

ADRIAN. If there's anything I can do you'll tell me, will you?

MARCUS (*to* SIGMUND). Does Maya know?

SIGMUND. She was going out.

MARCUS. I suppose she might as well. (*As a muted hope for alliance.*) But it won't help her getting excited.

SIGMUND. She will be calm, Maya is not foolish.

ADRIAN. Maybe we ought to get into it, Marcus – they wouldn't destroy the book, would they?

MARCUS (*a fragile laugh*). That's only one of several questions, Adrian – the first thing is to gather our thoughts. – Let me get your drink. (*He stands.*)

ADRIAN. I can wait with the drink, why don't we get into it?

MARCUS. All right. (*He sits again.*)

ADRIAN. Marcus?

MARCUS *turns to him. He points to the ceiling.* I know.

MARCUS *removes his gaze from* ADRIAN, *a certain mixture*

of embarrassment and resentment in his face.

Which doesn't mean I've drawn any conclusions about anyone. I mean that sincerely.

MARCUS. You understand, Adrian, that the scene here is not as uncomplicated as it may look from outside. You must believe me.

ADRIAN. I have no doubt about that, Marcus. But at the same time I wouldn't want to mislead you . . . (*He glances upwards.*) . . . or anyone else. If that book is destroyed or not returned to him – for whatever it's worth I intend to publicise what I believe is an act of barbarism. This is not some kind of an issue for me – this man is my brother.

Slight pause. MARCUS *is motionless. Then he turns to* AD-RIAN *and gestures to him to continue speaking, to amplify.* ADRIAN *looks atonished.* MARCUS *repeats the gesture even more imperatively.*

For example . . . I've always refused to peddle my books on television but there's at least two national network shows would be glad to have me, and for this I'd go on.

He stops; MARCUS *gestures to continue.*

Just telling the story of this evening would be hot news from coast to coast – including Washington, D.C. where some congressmen could easily decide we shouldn't sign any more trade bills with this country. And so on and so forth.

MARCUS. It was brandy, wasn't it?

ADRIAN (*still amazed*). . . Thanks, yes.

MARCUS *goes up to the drinks.* ADRIAN *catches* SIGMUND's *eye but the latter turns forward thoughtfully.* IRINA *enters, heading for the drinks.* MARCUS *brings* ADRIAN *a brandy as she makes herself a drink. In the continuing silence,* MARCUS *returns to the drink table, makes a whisky and takes it down to* SIGMUND. *Then . . .*

ADRIAN (*toward her, upstage*). So how's everything in Denmark?

IRINA (*pleasant laugh*). No-no, not everything.

ADRIAN (*thumbing to the ceiling – to* SIGMUND). *That* ought to keep them busy for a while.

MARCUS *chuckles, sits with his own drink.*

MARCUS. Cheers.

ADRIAN. Cheers.

SIGMUND. Cheers.

They drink. IRINA *brings a drink, sits on the floor beside* MARCUS.

MARCUS. Have you been to London this time?

ADRIAN (*slight pause. He glances toward* SIGMUND. *Then . . .*). No. How was London?

MARCUS. It's difficult there. It seems to be an endless strike.

ADRIAN (*waits a moment*). Yes.

He decides to continue.

Last time there my British publisher had emphysema and none of the elevators were working. I never heard so many Englishmen talking about a dictatorship before.

MARCUS. They probably have come to the end of it there. It's too bad, but why should evolution spare the English?

ADRIAN. Evolution toward what – Fascism?

MARCUS. Or the Arabs taking over more of the economy.

ADRIAN. I can see the bubble pipes in the House of Commons.

Laughter.

The Honorable Member from Damascus.

Laughter. It dies. ADRIAN *thumbs toward* SIGMUND *and then to the ceiling – addressing* MARCUS.

If they decide to give an answer, would it be tonight?

MARCUS (*turns up his palms . . . then . . .*) Relax, Adrian.

He drinks.

Please.

ADRIAN (*swallows a glassful of brandy*). This stuff really

spins the wheels. (*He inhales.*)

MARCUS. It comes from the mountains.

ADRIAN. I feel like I'm on one.

MARCUS. What's New York like now?

ADRIAN. New York? New York is another room in hell. (*Looking up.*) Of course not as architecturally ornate. In fact, a ceiling like this in New York – I can't imagine it lasting so long without some half-crooked writer climbing up and chopping holes in those cherubim.

MARCUS. The ceiling is nearly four hundred years old, you know.

ADRIAN. That makes it less frightful?

MARCUS. In a sense, maybe – for us it has some reassuring associations. When it was made, this city was the cultural capital of Europe – the world, really, this side of China. A lot of art, science, philosophy poured from this place.

ADRIAN. Painful.

MARCUS (*a conceding shrug*). But on the other hand, the government spends a lot keeping these in repair. It doesn't do to forget that, you know.

SIGMUND. That is true. They are repairing all the angels. It is very good to be an angel in our country.

MARCUS *smiles.*

Yes, we shall have the most perfect angels in the whole world.

MARCUS *laughs.*

But I believe perhaps every government is loving very much the angels, no, Adrian?

ADRIAN. Oh, no doubt about it. But six months under this particular kind of art and I'd be ready to cut my throat or somebody else's. What do you say we go to a bar, Marcus?

MARCUS (*to* SIGMUND). *Ezlatchu stau?*

SIGMUND (*he sighs, then nods*). *Ezlatchu.*

ADRIAN (*to* MARCUS). Where does that put us?

MARCUS. He doesn't mind staying till we've had something to eat. Afterwards, perhaps.

Pause. Silence.

ADRIAN. Let me in on it, Marcus – are we waiting for something?

MARCUS. No-no, I just thought we'd eat before we talked.

ADRIAN. Oh. All right.

IRINA (*patting her stomach*). I to sandwich?

MARCUS (*patting her head like a child's, laughing*). Maya is bringing very soon.

ADRIAN. She's as sweet as sugar, Marcus, where'd you find her?

MARCUS. Her husband is the head of Danish programming for the BBC. *There's* Maya.

He crosses to the corridor door.

ADRIAN. What does he do, loan her out?

MARCUS (*laughs*). No-no, she just wanted to see the country.

He exits into the corridor.

SIGMUND. And Marcus will show her every inch.

ADRIAN (*bursts out laughing*). Oh Sigmund, Sigmund – what a century! (*Sotto.*) What the hell is happening?

Men's shouting voices below, MAYA *yelling loudly.* MARCUS *instantly breaks into a run, disappears up the corridor.* ADRIAN *and* SIGMUND *listen. The shouting continues.* SIGMUND *gets up, goes and listens at the door.*

ADRIAN. What is it?

SIGMUND opens the door, goes into the corridor, listens.

Who are they?

A door is heard slamming below, silencing the shouts. Pause.

Sigmund?

SIGMUND comes back into the room.

What was it?

SIGMUND. Drunken men. They want to see the traitor to the motherland. Enemy of the working class.

He sits. Pause.

ADRIAN. . . . Come to my hotel.

SIGMUND. Is not possible. Be calm.

ADRIAN. How'd they know you were here?

SIGMUND *shrugs, then indicates the ceiling.*

They'd call out hoodlums?

SIGMUND *turns up his palms, shrugs.*

MARCUS *and* MAYA *appear up the corridor. She carries a large tray covered with a white cloth. He has a handkerchief to his cheekbone. He opens the door for her.* IRINA *stands and clears the marble table for the tray.* MARCUS *crosses to the Upstage Right doorway and exits.*

SIGMUND *stands.* MAYA *faces him across the room. Long pause.*

What happened?

MAYA (*with a gesture toward the food*). Come, poet.

SIGMUND *watches her for a moment more, then goes up to the food. She is staring excitedly into his face.*

The dark meat is goose.

SIGMUND *turns from her to the food.*

Adrian?

ADRIAN. I'm not hungry. Thanks.

MAYA (*she takes the plate from* SIGMUND *and loads it heavily*). Beer?

SIGMUND. I have whisky. You changed your haircut?

MAYA. From *Vogue* magazine. You like it?

SIGMUND. Very.

MAYA (*touching his face*). Very much, you say.

SIGMUND. Very, very much.

He returns to his chair with a loaded plate, sits and proceeds to eat in silence.

She pours herself a brandy, sits near him.

MAYA (*to* ADRIAN *as she watches* SIGMUND *admiringly*). He comes from the peasants, you know. That is why he is so beautiful. And he is sly. Like a snake.

Slight pause.

SIGMUND *eats.*

What have you done now? (*Indicates below.*) Why have they come?

SIGMUND *pauses in his eating, not looking at her.*

ADRIAN (*after the pause*). The cops took his manuscript to-night.

She inhales sharply with a gasp, nearly crying out. SIGMUND *continues to eat. She goes to him, embraces his head, mouth pressed to his hair.*

He draws her hands down, apparently warding off her emotion and continues eating. She moves and sits further away from him, staring ahead, alarmed and angry. MARCUS *enters from the bedroom, a bandage stuck to his cheekbone.*

MARCUS (*to* ADRIAN). Have you taken something?

ADRIAN. Not just yet, thanks.

MAYA *rises to confront* MARCUS *but, refusing her look, he passes her, a fixed smile on his face, picks up his drink from the marble table and comes downstage and stands. First he, then* ADRIAN, *then* MAYA *turn and watch* SIGMUND *eating. He eats thoroughly.* IRINA *is also eating, off by herself. Pause.*

MARCUS *goes to his chair, sits and lights a cigarette.* ADRIAN *watches him.*

It's like some kind of continuous crime.

MAYA. You are so rich, Adrian, so famous – why do you make such boring remarks?

ADRIAN. Because I am a bore.

MARCUS. Oh now, Maya . . .

MAYA (*sharply, to* MARCUS). Where is it not a continuous crime?

SIGMUND. It is the truth. (*To* ADRIAN.) Just so, yes. It is a continuous crime.

MAYA (*to the three*). Stupid. Like children. Stupid!

MARCUS. Sssh – take something to eat, dear . . .

ADRIAN. Why are we stupid?

Ignoring his question she goes up to the table, takes a goose
wing and bites into it. Then she comes down and stands eating.
After a moment . . .

MARCUS. It's wonderful to see you again, Adrian – what
brought you back?

MAYA. He has been talking to Allison Wolfe.

MARCUS (*smiling – to* ADRIAN). Oh, to Allison.

ADRIAN. Yes.

MARCUS. Is he still going around with that story?

MAYA. Yes.

MARCUS (*slight pause*). Adrian . . . you know, I'm sure, that
this house has been a sort of gathering place for writers for
many years now. And they've always brought their
girlfriends, and quite often met girls here they didn't
know before. Our first literary magazine after the war was
practically published from this room.

ADRIAN. I know that, Marcus.

MARCUS. Allison happened to be here one night, a month or
so ago, when there was a good bit of screwing going on.

ADRIAN. Sorry I missed it.

MARCUS. It *was* fairly spectacular. But believe me – it was
a purely spontaneous outburst of good spirits. Totally un-
expected, it was just one of those things that happens with
enough brandy.

ADRIAN *laughs*.

What I think happened is that – you see, we had a novelist
here who was about to emigrate; to put it bluntly, he is
paranoid. I can't blame him – he hasn't been able to publish here since the government changed. And I am one of
the people he blamed, as though I had anything to say
about who is or isn't to be published. But the fact that I

live decently and can travel proved to him that I have some
secret power with the higher echelons – in effect, that I
am some sort of agent.

ADRIAN. Those are understandable suspicions, Marcus.

MARCUS (*with a light laugh*). But why!

MAYA. It is marvellous, Adrian, how understandable everything is for you.

ADRIAN. I didn't say that at all, Maya; I know practically
nothing about Marcus so I could hardly be making an ac-
cusation, could I?

MARCUS. Of course not. It's only that the whole idea is so
appalling.

ADRIAN. Well, I apologise. But it's so underwater here an
outsider is bound to imagine all sorts of nightmares.

MAYA. You have no nightmares in America?

ADRIAN. You know me better than that, Maya – of course
we have them, but they're different.

IRINA (*revolving her finger*). Is music?

MARCUS. In a moment, dear.

MAYA. I really must say, Adrian – when you came here the
other times it was the Vietnam war, I believe. Did anyone
in this country blame you personally for it?

ADRIAN. No, they didn't. But it's not the same thing, Maya.

MAYA. It never is, is it?

ADRIAN. I was arrested twice for protesting the war. Not
that that means too much – we had lawyers to defend us
and the networks had it all over the country the next day.
So there's no comparison, and maybe I know it better than
most people. And that's why I'm not interested in blaming
anyone here. This is impossible, Marcus, why don't we
find a restaurant, I'm beginning to sound like an idiot.

MARCUS. We can't now, I've invited . . .

ADRIAN. Then why don't you meet us somewhere. Sigmund? What do you say, Maya – where's a good place?

MARCUS. Not tonight, Adrian.

> ADRIAN *turns to him, catching a certain obscure decision.*
> MARCUS *addresses* SIGMUND.

I took the liberty of asking Alexandra to stop by.

> SIGMUND *turns his head to him, surprised.* MAYA *turns to*
> MARCUS *from upstage, the plate in her hand.*

(*To* MAYA.) I thought he ought to talk to her. (*To* SIG-
MUND.) I hope you won't mind.

MAYA (*turns to* SIGMUND, *and with a certain surprise*).

You will talk with Alexandra?

> SIGMUND *is silent.*

IRINA (*revolving her finger*). Jazz?

MARCUS. In a moment, dear.

SIGMUND. She is coming?

MARCUS. She said she'd try. I think she will. (*To* ADRIAN.)
she is a great admirer of Sigmund's.

> MAYA *comes down to* ADRIAN *with a plate. She is watching*
> SIGMUND *who is facing front.*

MAYA. I think you should have asked if he agrees.

MARCUS. I don't see the harm. She can just join us for a
drink, if nothing more.

ADRIAN (*accepting the plate*). Thanks. She a writer?

MAYA. Her father is the Minister of Interior. (*Pointing at the
ceiling.*)

He is in charge . . .

ADRIAN. Oh! I see.

> *He turns to watch* SIGMUND *who is facing front.*

MARCUS. She writes poetry.

MAYA. Yes. (*Glances anxiously to* SIGMUND.) Tremendous .
. . (*She spreads her arms.*). . . long poems.

> *She takes a glass and drinks deeply.*

MARCUS (*on the verge of sharpness*).

Nevertheless, I think she has a certain talent.

MAYA. Yes. You think she has a certain talent, Sigmund?

MARCUS. Now Maya . . .

He reaches out and lifts the glass out of her hand.

MAYA. Each year, you see, Adrian – since her father was appointed, this woman's poetry is more and more admired by more and more of our writers. A few years ago only a handful appreciated her, but now practically everybody calls her a master. (*Proudly.*) Excepting for Sigmund – until now, anyway.

She takes the glass from where MARCUS *placed it.*

SIGMUND (*a pause*). She is not to my taste, (*He hesitates.*) but perhaps she is a good poet.

MAYA (*slight pause*). But she has very thick legs.

MARCUS *turns to her.*

But that must be said, Marcus . . . (*She laughs.*) We are not yet obliged to overlook a fact of nature. Please say she has thick legs.

MARCUS. I have no interest in her legs.

MAYA. Sigmund, my darling – surely you will say she . . .

MARCUS. Stop that, Maya . . .

MAYA (*suddenly, at the top of her voice*). It is important! (*She turns to* SIGMUND.)

SIGMUND. She has thick legs, yes.

MAYA. Yes. (*She presses his head to her hip.*) Some truths will not change, and certain people, for all our sakes, are appointed never to forget them. How do the Jews say? – If I forget thee, O Jerusalem, may I cut off my hand . . . ? (*To* IRINA.) You want jazz?

IRINA (*starts to rise, happily*). Jazz!

MAYA (*helping her up*). Come, you poor girl, we have hundreds . . . I mean he does. (*She laughs.*) My God, Marcus, how long I lived here. (*She laughs, nearly weeping.*) I'm going crazy . . .

SIGMUND (*stands*). I must walk. I have eaten too much. (*He buttons his jacket.*)

ADRIAN (*indicating below*). What about those men?

SIGMUND beckons ADRIAN *toward the doorway Left.*
He moves toward the left door, which he opens as ADRIAN
stands, starts after him, then halts and turns with uncertainty
to MARCUS *and* MAYA *who look on without expression.*
ADRIAN *goes out, shutting the door.* SIGMUND *is standing*
in the corridor.

MAYA. (*to* IRINA). Come, we have everything. (*She goes and*
opens an overhead cabinet revealing hundreds of records.)
From Paris, London, New York, Rio . . . you like Conga?
IRINA *reads the labels.* MAYA *turns her head toward the cor-*
ridor. MARCUS *now turns as well.*

SIGMUND. Do you understand?

ADRIAN. No.

SIGMUND. I am to be arrested.

ADRIAN. How do you know that?

SIGMUND. Alexandra is the daughter of . . .

ADRIAN. I know – the Minister of . . .

SIGMUND. Marcus would never imagine I would meet with
this woman otherwise.

ADRIAN. Why? What's she about?

SIGMUND. She is collecting the dead for her father. She ar-
range for writers to go before the television, and apologise
for the government. Mea Culpa – to kissing their ass.
Slight pause.

ADRIAN. I think you've got to leave the country, Sigmund.
MAYA *crosses the room.*

SIGMUND. Is impossible. We cannot discuss it.
MAYA *enters the corridor, closing the door behind her.*

MAYA. Get out.

SIGMUND (*he comes to her, takes her hand gently*). I must talk
to Adrian.

MAYA. Get out, get out! (*To* ADRIAN.) He must leave the
country. (*To* SIGMUND.) Finish with it! Tell Marcus.

SIGMUND (*turns her to the door, a hand on her back. He opens the door for her*). Please, Maya.

(*She enters the room glancing back at him in terror. He shuts the door.*)

IRINA (*holding out a record*). Play?

MAYA *looks to* MARCUS *who turns away. Then she goes and uncovers a record player, turns it on, sets the record on it. During the following the music plays, a jazz piece or Conga. First* IRINA *dances by herself, then gets* MARCUS *up and dances with him.* MAYA *sits, drinking.*

Pause.

SIGMUND. You have a pistol?

ADRIAN. . . . A pistol?

SIGMUND. Yes.

ADRIAN. No. Of course not. (*Pause.*) How could I carry a pistol on an airplane?

SIGMUND. Why not? He has one in his valise. I saw it.

Pause.

ADRIAN. What good would a pistol do?

Pause.

SIGMUND. . . . It is very difficult to get pistol in this country.

ADRIAN. This is unreal, Sigmund, you can't be thinking of a . . .

SIGMUND. If you will engage him in conversation, I will excuse myself to the bathroom. He has put his valise in the bedroom. I will take it from the valise.

ADRIAN. And do what with it?

SIGMUND. I will keep it, and he will tell them that I have it. In this case they will not arrest me.

ADRIAN. But why not?

SIGMUND. They will avoid at the present time to shoot me.

ADRIAN. . . . And I'm to do . . . what am I to . . . ?

SIGMUND. It is nothing; you must only engage him when I am excusing myself to the bathroom. Come . . .

ADRIAN. Let me catch my breath, will you? . . . It's unreal to me, Sigmund, I can't believe you have to do this.

SIGMUND. It is not dangerous, believe me.

ADRIAN. Not for me, but I have a passport. – Then this is why Marcus came back?

SIGMUND. I don't know. He has many friend in the government, but . . . I don't know why.

ADRIAN. He's an agent.

SIGMUND. Is possible not.

ADRIAN. Then what is he?

SIGMUND. Marcus is Marcus.

ADRIAN. Please, explain to me. I've got to understand before I go in there.

SIGMUND. It is very complicated between us.

ADRIAN. Like what? Maya?

SIGMUND. Maya also. (*Slight pause.*) When I was young writer, Marcus was the most famous novelist in our country. In Stalin time he has six years in prison. He cannot write. I was not in prison. When he has returned I am very popular, but he was forgotten. It is tragic story.

ADRIAN. You mean he's envious of you.

SIGMUND. This is natural.

ADRIAN. But didn't you say he's protected you . . .

SIGMUND. Yes, of course. Marcus is very complicated man.

ADRIAN. But with all that influence, why can't you sit down and maybe he can think of something for you.

SIGMUND. He has thought of something – he has thought of Alexandra.

ADRIAN. You mean he's trying to destroy you.

SIGMUND. No. Is possible he believes he is trying to help me.

ADRIAN. But subconsciously . . .

SIGMUND. Yes. Come, we must go back.

ADRIAN. Just one more minute. You're convinced he's not an agent.

SIGMUND. My opinion, no.

ADRIAN. But how does he get all these privileges?

SIGMUND. Marcus is lazy. Likewise, he is speaking French, English, German – five-six language. When the foreign writers are coming, he is very gentleman, he makes amusing salon, he is showing the castles, the restaurants, introduce beautiful girls. When these writers return home they say is no bad problem in this civilised country. He makes very nice impression, and for this they permit him to be lazy. Is not necessary to be agent.

ADRIAN. You don't think it's possible that he learned they were going to arrest you, and came back to help you?

SIGMUND *looks at him, surprised.*

That makes as much sense as anything else, Sigmund. Could he have simply wanted to do something decent? Maybe I'm being naive, but if he wanted your back broken his best bet would be just to sit tight in London and let it happen.

SIGMUND *is silent.*

And as for calling Alexandra – maybe he figured your only chance *is* actually to make peace with the government.

SIGMUND *is silent.*

You grab that gun and you foreclose everything – you're an outlaw. Is it really impossible to sit down with Marcus, man to man? I mean you're pinning everything on an interpretation, aren't you?

SIGMUND. I know Marcus.

ADRIAN. Sigmund – every conversation I've ever had with him about this country, he's gone out of his way to praise you – your talent and you personally. I can't believe I was taken in, he genuinely admires your guts, your resistance. Let me call him out here.

SIGMUND *turns, uncertain but alarmed.*

What's to lose? Maybe there's a string he can pull, let's

put *his* feet to the fire. Because he's all over Europe lamenting conditions here, he's a big liberal in Europe. I've seen him get girls with those lamentations. Let me call him on it.

SIGMUND (*a blossoming suspicion in the corners of his eyes*). I will never make speech on the television . . .

ADRIAN (*alarmed*). For Christ's sake, Sigmund, you don't imagine *I* would want that. (*Exploding.*) This is a quagmire, a fucking asylum! . . . But I'm not helping out with any guns. It's suicide, you'll have to do that alone.

He goes to the door.

SIGMUND. Adrian?

ADRIAN. I'm sorry, Sigmund, but that's the way I feel.

SIGMUND. I want my manuscript, if you wish to talk to Marcus, I have nothing to object . . . on this basis.

ADRIAN *looks at him, unsatisfied, angry. He turns and flings the door open, enters the room.*

ADRIAN. Marcus? Can I see you minute?

MARCUS. Of course. What is it?

ADRIAN. Out here, please . . . if you don't mind?

MARCUS *crosses the room and enters the corridor.* ADRIAN *shuts the door.*

SIGMUND *avoids* MARCUS's *eyes, stands waiting.* MARCUS *turns to* ADRIAN *as he shuts the door.*

MARCUS. Yes?

MAYA *opens the door, enters the corridor, shuts it behind her.* MARCUS *turns up his robe collar.*

ADRIAN (*breaks into an embarrassed grin*). I'm not sure what to say or not say . . . I'm more of a stranger than I'd thought, Marcus . . .

MARCUS. We're all strangers in this situation – nobody ever learns how to deal with it.

ADRIAN. . . . I take it you have some contacts with the government.

MARCUS. Many of us do; it's a small country.

ADRIAN. I think they ought to know that ah . . . (*He glances to* SIGMUND, *but* SIGMUND *is not facing in his direction.*) if he's to be arrested, he'll – resist.

MAYA *turns quickly to* SIGMUND, *alarm in her face.*

MARCUS. I don't understand – (*To* SIGMUND, *with a faintly embarrassed grin.*) Why couldn't you have said that to me?

SIGMUND, *bereft of an immediate answer, starts to turn to him.*

Well, it doesn't matter. (*He is flushed. Turning back to* AD-RIAN.) Yes?

ADRIAN. What I thought was, that . . .

MARCUS. Of course, if we're talking about some – violent gesture, they will advertise it as the final proof he is insane. Which is what they've claimed all along. But what was your thought?

ADRIAN. I have the feeling that the inevitable is being accepted. They act and you react. I'd like to sit down, the four of us, and see if we can come up with some out that nobody's ever thought of before.

MARCUS. Certainly. But it's a waste of time if you think you can change their programme.

ADRIAN. Which is what, exactly.

MARCUS. Obviously – to drive him out of the country. Failing that, to make it impossible for him to function.

ADRIAN. And you think?

MARCUS. There's no question in my mind – he must emigrate. They've taken the work of his last five years, what more do you want?

ADRIAN. There's no one at all you could approach?

MARCUS. With what? What can I offer that they need?

ADRIAN. Like what, for example?

MARCUS. Well, if he agreed to emigrate, conceivably they might let go of the manuscript. – Providing, of course, that it isn't too politically inflammatory. But that could be dealt with, I think – they badly want him gone.

ADRIAN. There's no one up there who could be made to understand that if they ignored him he would simply be another novelist . . .

MARCUS (*laughing lightly*). But will he ignore *them*? How is it possible? This whole country is inside his skin – that is his greatness – They have a right to be terrified.

ADRIAN. Supposing there were a copy of the manuscript.

MARCUS. But there isn't, so it's pointless talking about it.

ADRIAN. But if there were.

MARCUS. It might have been a consideration.

ADRIAN. . . . If they knew it would be published abroad.

MARCUS. It might slow them down, yes. But they know Sigmund's personality.

ADRIAN. How do you mean?

MARCUS. He's not about to trust another person with his fate – it's a pity; they'd never have found it in this house in a hundred years. The cellar's endless, the gallery upstairs full of junk – to me, this is the saddest part of all. If it had made a splash abroad it might have held their hand for six months, perhaps longer. (*With a regretful glance at* SIGMUND.) But . . . so it goes.

Pause. He blows on his hands.

It's awfully cold out here, come inside . . .

He starts for the door.

ADRIAN. There's a copy in Paris.

MAYA *and* SIGMUND *turn swiftly to him.*

MARCUS. . . . In Paris.

ADRIAN. I sent it off this morning.

MARCUS. *This* morning?

ADRIAN. I ran into a cousin of mine; had no idea she was here. She took it with her to Gallimard – they're my publishers.

MARCUS (*a broken smile emerges; he is filling with a swirl of colours, glancing first at* MAYA, *then at* SIGMUND, *then back to* ADRIAN). Well then . . . that much is solved.

He goes to the door.

ADRIAN. They should be told, don't you think?

MARCUS (*he stands at the door, his hand on the knob. Finally he turns to all of them*). How terrible. (*Slight pause. To* MAYA *and* SIGMUND.) *Such* contempt. (*Slight pause.*) Why? . . . Can you tell me?

They avoid his gaze. He turns to ADRIAN.

There's no plane to Paris today. Monday, Wednesday and Friday. This is Tuesday, Adrian.

SIGMUND. I did not ask him to say that.

MARCUS. But perfectly willing to stand there and hope I'd believe it.

ADRIAN. I'm sorry, Marcus . . .

MARCUS (*laughing*). But Adrian, I couldn't care less.

MAYA (*moving to him*). Help him.

MARCUS. Absolutely not. I am finished with it. No one will ever manipulate me, I will not be in that position.

MAYA. He is a stupid man, he understands nothing!

ADRIAN. Now hold it a second . . .

MAYA. Get out of here!

ADRIAN. Just hold it a second, Goddammit! I'm out of my depth, Marcus, but I've apologised. I'm sorry. But you have to believe it was solely my invention, Sigmund has absolute faith in you.

SIGMUND. You can forgive him, Marcus – he tells you the truth; he believes you are my friend, he said this to me a moment ago.

ADRIAN. I feel he's drowning, Marcus, it was just something to grab for. (*He holds out his hand.*) Forgive me, it just popped out of my mouth.

MARCUS (*silently clasps his hand for an instant, and lets go. To*

SIGMUND *and* MAYA *especially*). Come inside. We'll talk.

ADRIAN (*as* MARCUS *turns to the door*). . . . Marcus?

MARCUS *turns to him. He is barely able to continue.*

Don't you think – it would be wiser – a bar, or something?

MARCUS. I'm expecting Alexandra.

ADRIAN. Could you leave a note on the door? But it's up to you and Sigmund. (*To* SIGMUND.) What do you think?

SIGMUND (*hesitates*). It is for Marcus to decide – (*He looks at* MARCUS.) – it is his house.

MARCUS *expressionless, stands silent.*

MAYA. Darling . . . (*delicately*.) . . . it will endure a thousand years. (MARCUS *looks at her.*) . . . I've read it. It is all we ever lived. They must not, must not touch it. Whatever humiliation, whatever is necessary for this book, yes. More than he himself, more than any human being – this book they cannot harm. – Francesco's is still open. (*She turns to* ADRIAN.) But I must say to you, Adrian – nothing has ever been found in there. Or in this house. We have looked everywhere.

ADRIAN. It's entirely up to Marcus. (*To* MARCUS.) You feel it's all right to talk in there?

Long pause.

MARCUS (*his resentment*). I think Maya has answered that question, don't you?

ADRIAN. Okay. Then you're not sure.

MARCUS. But you are, apparently.

ADRIAN (*slight pause. To* SIGMUND). I think I ought to leave.

SIGMUND. No-no . . .

ADRIAN. I think I'm only complicating it for you –

SIGMUND. I insist you stay . . .

ADRIAN (*laughs nervously, his arm touching* SIGMUND's *shoulder*). I'm underwater, kid, I can't operate when I'm drowning. (*Without pausing, to* MARCUS.) I don't understand why you're offended.

MARCUS. But the question has been answered once. There has never been any proof of an installation here. But when so many writers congregate here I've had to assume there might be something. The fact is, I have always warned people to be careful what they say in there – but only to be on the safe side. Is that enough?

SIGMUND. Come! (*To* MARCUS, *heartily, as he begins to press* ADRIAN *towards the door.*) Now I will have one big whisky . . .

MARCUS *laughs, starting for the door.*

ADRIAN (*separating himself from* SIGMUND). I'll see you tomorrow, Sigmund.

Silence. They go still.

This is all your marbles, kid. It's too important for anyone to be standing on his dignity. I think I'm missing some of the overtones. (*To* MARCUS.) but all I know is that if it were me I'd feel a lot better if I could hear you say what you just said – but in there.

MARCUS. What *I* said?

ADRIAN (*slight pause*). . . . . That you've always warned people that the government might be listening, in that room.

SIGMUND. Is not necessary . . .

ADRIAN. I think it . . .

SIGMUND. Absolutely not! – Please . . .

He presses ADRIAN *toward the door, and stretching his hand out to* MARCUS. . .

Come, Marcus, please.

SIGMUND *leads the way into the room, followed by* ADRIAN, *then* MARCUS *and* MAYA. *For an instant they are all awkwardly standing there. Then, pressing his hand against his stomach . . .*

Excuse me one moment.

He goes up toward the bedroom doorway.

ADRIAN (*suddenly alerted. He starts after* SIGMUND). Sigmund . . .

But SIGMUND *is gone. He is openly conflicted about rushing after him . . .*

MAYA. What is it?

ADRIAN (*blurting, in body-shock*). Level with him. Marcus . . . this is your Hemingway, your Faulkner, for Christ's sake – help him!

SIGMUND enters from bedroom, a pistol in his hand. IRINA, *seeing it, strides away from him in fright.*

SIGMUND (*to* MARCUS). Forgive me. I must have it. (*He puts it in his pocket*).

IRINA (*pointing at his pocket*). Shoot?

SIGMUND. No-no. We are all friend. *Alle gute Freunde hier.*

IRINA. Ah.

She turns questioningly to MARCUS. *Then* ADRIAN, MAYA *and* SIGMUND. *A pause.*

ADRIAN. Marcus?

MARCUS, *at centre, turns front, anger mounting in his face.* MAYA *goes and shuts off the record player. Then she turns to him, waiting.*

Will you say it? In here? Please?

Curtain.

Act Two

Positions the same. A tableau, MARCUS *at centre, all waiting for him to speak. Finally he moves, glances at* SIGMUND.

MARCUS. They are preparing a trial for you.

MAYA (*clapping her hands together, crying out*). Marcus!
   She starts toward him but he walks from her, turning away in impatience. She halts.
   When?

   MARCUS *is silent, downing his resentment.*
   Do you know when?

MARCUS. I think within the month.

MAYA (*turning to* SIGMUND). My God, my God.

SIGMUND (*after a moment*). And Otto and Peter?

MARCUS. I don't know about them.
   He goes in the silence to his chair, sits. A pause.

ADRIAN. What would they charge him with?

MARCUS. . . . Fantastic. Break off a trip, fly across Europe, and now I'm asked – what am I asked? – to justify myself? Is that it?
   Unable to answer, ADRIAN *evades his eyes, then glances to* SIGMUND *for aid; but* SIGMUND *is facing front and now walks to a chair and sits.*

MAYA (*to* MARCUS). No-no, Dear . . . (*Of* SIGMUND.) It's a shock for him . . .

MARCUS (*rejecting her apology he glances at* ADRIAN). . . . Section 19, I'd imagine. Slandering the state.

ADRIAN. On what grounds?

MARCUS. He's been sending out some devastating letters to the European press; this last one to the United Nations – have you read that?

ADRIAN. Just now in Paris, yes.

MARCUS. What'd you think of it?

ADRIAN (*with a cautious glance at* SIGMUND). It was pretty hot, I guess – What's the penalty for that?

MARCUS. A year. Two, three, five – who knows?

Slight pause.

MAYA. It was good of you to return, dear.

MARCUS *does not respond. She invites* SIGMUND's *gratitude.*

. . . Sigmund?

SIGMUND (*he waits an instant*). Yes. Thank you, Marcus. (MARCUS *remains looking front.*) It is definite?

MARCUS. I think it is. And it will affect every writer in the country, if it's allowed to happen.

SIGMUND. How do you know this?

Slight pause.

MARCUS. My publisher had a press reception for me day before yesterday – for my book. A fellow from our London embassy turned up. We chatted for a moment, then I forgot about him, but in the street afterwards, he was suddenly beside me . . . we shared a cab.

Slight pause. He turns directly to SIGMUND.

He said he was from the Embassy Press Section.

SIGMUND. Police.

MARCUS (*he lowers his eyes in admission*). He was . . . quite violent . . . his way of speaking.

SIGMUND. About me.

Slight pause.

MARCUS. I haven't heard that kind of language . . . since . . . the old days. 'You are making a mistake,' he said, 'if you think we need tolerate this scum any longer . . .'

MAYA. My God, my God . . .

MARCUS. 'You can do your friend a favour,' he said, 'and tell him to get out this month or he will eat his own shit for five or six years.'

MAYA *weeps.*

'And as far as a protest in the West, he can wrap it in bacon fat and shove it up his ass.' Pounded the seat with his fist. Bloodshot eyes. I thought he was going to hit me for a moment there . . . it was quite an act.

ADRIAN. An act?

MARCUS. Well he wasn't speaking for himself, of course.

Slight pause.

I started a letter, but I know your feelings about leaving – I felt we had to talk about it face to face.

SIGMUND. Please.

MARCUS (*he hesitates, then turns to* ADRIAN). Are you here as a journalist?

ADRIAN. God, no – I just thought I'd stop by . . .

MAYA. He has written a novel about us.

MARCUS (*unguarded*). About us? Really . . . !

ADRIAN. Well not literally . . .

MARCUS. When is it coming out?

ADRIAN. It won't. I've abandoned it.

MARCUS. Oh! That's too bad. Why?

ADRIAN. I'm not here to write about you, Marcus . . . honestly. MARCUS *nods, unconvinced. To* SIGMUND *as well.*) I'll leave now if you think I'm in the way . . .

SIGMUND *doesn't react.*

MARCUS. It's all right.

Slight pause.

But if you decide to write something about us . . .

ADRIAN. I've no intention . . .

MARCUS (*smiling*). You never know. We have a tactical disagreement, Sigmund and I. To me, it's really a question of having had different experiences – although there are only seven or eight years between us; things that he finds intolerable are actually – from another viewpoint – improvements over the past . . .

ADRIAN (*indicating* MAYA). I only found out today you were

in prison . . .

MARCUS. A camp, actually – we dug coal.

ADRIAN. Six years.

MARCUS. And four months.

ADRIAN. What for?

MARCUS. It's one of those stories which, although long, is not interesting. (*He laughs.*) The point is simple, in any case – We happen to occupy a . . . strategic zone, really – between two hostile ways of life. And no government here is free to do what it would like to do. But some intelligent, sympathetic people are up there now who weren't around in the old times, and to challenge these people, to even insult them is to indulge in a sort of fantasy . . .

SIGMUND (*pointing to the ceiling*). Marcus, this is reality?

MARCUS. Let me finish . . .

SIGMUND. But is very important – who is fantastic?

He laughs.

We are some sort of characters in a poem which they are writing; is not my poem, is their poem . . . and I do not like this poem, it makes me crazy!

He laughs.

ADRIAN. I understand what he means, though . . .

SIGMUND. I not! I am sorry. Excuse me, Marcus – please continue.

MARCUS (*slight pause*). They ought not be forced into political trials again . . .

SIGMUND. *I* am forcing . . . ?

MARCUS. May I finish? It will mean a commitment which they will have to carry through, willingly or not. And that can only mean turning out the lights for all of us, and for a long time to come. It mustn't be allowed to happen, Sigmund. And it need not happen. (*Slight pause.*) I think you have to get out. For all our sakes.

With an ironic shake of his head, SIGMUND *makes a long*

exhale.

MARCUS. . . . I've called Alexandra because I think you need a line of communication now. If only to stall things for a time, or whatever you . . .

SIGMUND (*toward* MAYA). I must now communicate with *Alexandra*.

MARCUS. She adores your work, whatever you think of her.

SIGMUND *gives him a sarcastic glance.*

This splendid isolation has to end, Sigmund – it was never real and now it's impossible.

SIGMUND (*shakes his head*). I will wait for her. – I may wait?

MARCUS. I certainly hope you will. (*Slight pause.*) I only ask you to keep in mind that this goes beyond your personal feelings about leaving . . .

SIGMUND. I have never acted for personal feelings.

MARCUS (*insistently*). You've been swept away now and then – that United Nations letter could change nothing except enrage them . . .

SIGMUND. I may not also be enraged?

MAYA. Don't argue about it, please . . .

SIGMUND (*smiling to her*). Perhaps is time we argue . . .

MAYA. Sigmund, we are all too old to be right!

She picks up a glass.

MARCUS. Are you getting drunk?

MAYA. No, I am getting sorry. Is no one to be sorry? I am sorry for both of you. I am sorry for Socialism. I am sorry for Marx and Engels and Lenin – (*She shouts to the air.*) I am sorry! (*To* IRINA, *irritably.*) Don't be frightened. (*She pours a drink.*)

A pause.

ADRIAN. I'd like to take back what I asked you before, Marcus.

MARCUS. How can I know what is in this room? How ludicrous can you get?

ADRIAN. I agree. I wouldn't be willing to answer that question in my house either.

SIGMUND. But would not be necessary to ask such question in your house.

ADRIAN. Oh, don't kid yourself . . .

MARCUS. The FBI is everywhere . . .

ADRIAN. Not everywhere, but they get around. The difference with us is that it's illegal.

SIGMUND. *Vive la différence.*

MARCUS. Provided you catch them.

ADRIAN (*laughs*). Right.

He catches SIGMUND'S *dissatisfaction with him.*

I'm not saying it's the same . . .

SIGMUND (*turns away from* ADRIAN *to* MAYA). Please, Maya, a whisky.

MAYA (*eagerly*). Yes!

She goes up to the drink table. Silence. She pours a drink, brings it to SIGMUND.

ADRIAN. Did this woman say what time she . . . ?

MARCUS. She's at some embassy dinner. As soon as she can break away. Shouldn't be long. (*Slight pause. Indicating* SIGMUND'S *pocket.*) Give me that thing, will you?

SIGMUND *does not respond.*

ADRIAN. Go ahead, Sigmund.

SIGMUND. I . . . keep for few minutes. (*He drinks. A pause.*)

ADRIAN. I'm exhausted. (*He hangs his head and shakes it.*)

MAYA. You drink too fast.

ADRIAN. No . . . it's the whole thing – it suddenly hit me. (*He squeezes his eyes.*) Mind if I lie down?

MARCUS (*gesturing toward the couch*). Of course.

ADRIAN *goes to the couch.*

What's *your* feeling?

ADRIAN. He's got to get out, I've told him that. (*Lying down.*) They're doing great, what do they need literature for? It's a pain in the ass. (*He throws an arm over his eyes, sighs.*) Christ . . . it's unbelievable. An hour from the Sorbonne.

MAYA (*a long pause; she sits between* SIGMUND *and* MAYA, *glancing uncomfortably from one to the other*). It was raining in London?

MARCUS. No, surprisingly warm. – How's your tooth?

MAYA (*pointing to a front tooth, showing him*). They saved it.

MARCUS. Good. He painted the bathroom.

MAYA. Yes, he came, finally. I paid him. The rest of the money is in the desk.

MARCUS. Thanks, dear. Looks very nice.
Slight pause.

MAYA (*she leans her elbow on her knee, her chin on her fist, she observes her leg, then glances at* MARCUS). My bird died on Sunday.

MARCUS. Really? Lulu?

MAYA. Yes. I finally found out, though – she was a male. (*To* SIGMUND.) And all these years I called him Lulu!

SIGMUND. I can give you one of my rabbits.

MAYA. Oh my God, no rabbits. (*She sighs.*) No birds, no cats, no dogs . . . Nothing, nothing anymore.
She drinks. A pause.

ADRIAN (*from the couch*). You ever get mail from your programme?

MAYA. Oh very much. Mostly for recipes, sometimes I teach them to cook.

SIGMUND. She is very comical. She is marvellous actress.

ADRIAN. It's not a political . . . ?

MAYA. No! It's too early in the morning. I hate politics . . . boring, boring, always the same . . . You know something? You are both very handsome.
They both look at her and laugh softly.
You too, Adrian.

She looks at her glass.

And this is wonderful whisky.

ADRIAN. Not too much, dear.

MAYA. No-no.

She gets up with her glass, moves toward the window at Right.
There was such a marvellous line – that English poet, what
was his name? Very famous . . . you published him in the
first or second issue, I think . . . 'The world . . .'

She presses her forehead – MARCUS *observes her and she sees
him.*

I'm not drunk, it's only so long ago. Oh yes! 'The world
needs a wash and a week's rest.'

ADRIAN. Auden.

MAYA. Auden, yes! – a wash and week's rest – what a wonderful solution.

ADRIAN. Yeah – last one into the Ganges is a rotten egg.

They laugh.

MARCUS. Every now and then you sound like Brooklyn.

ADRIAN. That's because I come from Philadelphia. How do
you know about Brooklyn?

MARCUS. I was in the American Army.

ADRIAN (*amazed, sits up*). How do you come to the American
Army?

MAYA. He was sergeant.

MARCUS. I enlisted in London – we had to get out when the
Nazis came. I was translator and interpreter for General
McBride, First Army Intelligence.

ADRIAN. Isn't that funny? – every once in a while you come
into a kind of – focus, that's very familiar. I've never understood it.

MARCUS. I was in almost three years.

ADRIAN. Huh! (*He laughs.*) I don't know why I'm so glad to
hear it . . .

MARCUS. Well, you can place me now – we all want that.

ADRIAN. I guess so. What'd she mean, that you published Auden?

MAYA. Marcus was the editor of the magazine, until they closed it.

ADRIAN (*toward* SIGMUND). I didn't know that.

SIGMUND. Very good editor – Marcus was first editor who accept to publish my story.

MAYA. If it had been in English – or even French or Spanish – our magazine would have been as famous as the *New Yorker*.

MARCUS (*modestly*). Well . . .

MAYA (*to* MARCUS). In my opinion it was better . . . (*To* ADRIAN.) But our language even God doesn't read. People would stand on line in the street downstairs, like for bread. People from factories, soldiers from the army, professors . . . It was like some sort of Bible, every week a new prophecy. Pity you missed it . . .

It was like living on a ship – every morning there was a different island.

MARCUS (*to* SIGMUND – *a gesture of communication*). Elizabeth didn't look well, is she all right?

SIGMUND. She was very angry tonight. She is sometimes foolish.

Slight pause.

MAYA. Could he live, in America?

ADRIAN. I'm sure he could. Universities'd be honoured to have him.

SIGMUND. I am speaking English like six years-old child.

ADRIAN. Faculty wives'll be overjoyed to correct you. You'd be a big hit – with all that hair.

SIGMUND (*laughs dryly*). You are not going to Algeria?

MARCUS. On Friday.

ADRIAN. What's in Algeria?

MARCUS. There's a writers' congress – they've asked me to go.

ADRIAN. Communist countries?

MARCUS. Yes. But it's a big one – Arabs, Africans, Latin Americans . . . the lot.

SIGMUND. The French?

MARCUS. Some French, yes – Italians, too, I think.

ADRIAN. What do you do at those things?

MAYA (*admiringly*). He represents our country – he lies on the beach with a gin and tonic.

MARCUS (*laughs*). It's too cold for the beach now.

(*To* ADRIAN.) They're basically ideological discussions.

SIGMUND. Boring, no?

MARCUS. Agony. But there are some interesting people, sometimes.

SIGMUND. You can speak of us there?

MARCUS (*turns to him, silent, unable to answer*). No?

MARCUS. We're not on the agenda.

MAYA. It's difficult, dear . . .

SIGMUND. But perhaps privately – to the Italian comrades? . . . French? Perhaps they would be interested for my manuscript.

MARCUS *nods positively, but turns up his palms – he'll do what he can.*

(*With the slightest edge of sarcasm.*)

You will see, perhaps.

He chucks his head, closes his eyes with his face stretched upward, his hand tapping frustratedly on his chair arm, his foot beating.

So-so-so-so.

MARCUS (*looking front*). The important thing . . . is to be useful.

SIGMUND (*flatly, without irony*). Yes, always. (*Slight pause.*) Thank you, that you have returned for this, I am grateful.

MARCUS. Whatever you decide, it ought to be soon. Once they move to prosecute . . .

SIGMUND. Yes. I have still some questions – we can take a walk later, perhaps.

MARCUS. All right. I've told you all I know . . .

SIGMUND. . . . About ourselves.

MARCUS (*surprised*). Oh. All right.

Pause.

MAYA. How handsome you all are! I must say . . .

MARCUS *laughs – she persists.*

Really, it's unusual for writers. (*Suddenly to* IRINA.) And she is so lovely . . . *Du bist sehr schöne.*

IRINA. *Danke.*

MAYA (*to* MARCUS). Isn't she very young?

MARCUS (*shrugs.*) We only met two days ago.

MAYA (*touching his hair*). How marvellous. You are like God, darling – you can always create new people. (*She laughs, and with sudden energy . . .*) Play something, Sigmund . . . ! (*She goes to* SIGMUND *to get him up.*)

Come . . .

SIGMUND. No-no-no . . .

MAYA (*she suddenly bends and kisses the top of his head. Her eyes fill with tears*). Don't keep that thing . . . (*She reaches for his pocket; he takes her hand and pats it, looking up at her. She stares down at him.*) The day he walked in here for the first time . . . (*Glancing at* MARCUS.) Do you remember? The snow was half a metre high on his hat – I thought he was a peasant selling potatoes, he bowed the snow all over my typewriter. (*Glancing at* ADRIAN.) And he takes out this lump of paper – it was rolled up like a bomb. A story full of colours, like a painting; this boy from the beet fields – a writer! It was a miracle – such prose from a field of beets. That morning – for half an hour – I believed Socialism. For half an hour I . . .

MARCUS (*cutting her off*). What brings you back, Adrian?

The telephone rings in the bedroom.

Probably for you.

MAYA. For me? (*Going toward the bedroom.*) I can't imagine . . . (*She exits.*)

ADRIAN. I don't really know why I came. There's always been something here that I . . .

IRINA (*getting up, pointing to the piano*). I may?

MARCUS. Certainly . . . please.

IRINA *sits at the piano.*

SIGMUND. I think you will write your book again.

ADRIAN. I doubt it – there's a kind of music here that escapes me. I really don't think I dig you people.

IRINA (*testing the piano, she runs a scale; it is badly out of tune and she makes a face, turning to* MARCUS). Ach . . .

MARCUS (*apologising*). I'm sorry, it's too old to be tuned anymore . . . but go ahead . . .

MAYA *enters.*

MAYA. There's no one – they cut off.

SIGMUND *turns completely around to her, alerted.*

MAYA (*to him, reassuringly*). I'm sure they'll call back . . . it was an accident. Good! You play?

IRINA *launches into a fast 'Bei Meir Bist Du Schön', the strings whining . . .*

MAYA. Marvellous! Jitterbug! (*She breaks into a jitterbug with her glass in one hand, lifting her skirt . . .*

Come on, Adrian . . . !

She starts for ADRIAN, *but* IRINA *stops playing and stands up pushing her fingers into her ears.*

IRINA. Is too, too . . .

MAYA. No, play, play . . .

IRINA (*refusing, laughing, as she descends onto the carpet beside* MARCUS, *shutting her ears*). Please, please, please . . .

MARCUS (*patting* IRINA). I believe she's done concerts . . . serious music.

He looks at his watch – then to SIGMUND.

You're not going outside with that thing, are you?

SIGMUND *glances at him.*

It's absurd.

MAYA. It must be the Americans – ever since they started building that hotel the phones keep ringing.

ADRIAN. What hotel?

MAYA. The Hilton . . . three blocks from here. It's disarranged the telephones.

MARCUS. I'd love to read your novel – do you have it with you?

ADRIAN. It's no good.

MARCUS. That's surprising – what's the problem?

ADRIAN (*sits up*). Well . . . I started out with a bizarre, exotic quality. People sort of embalmed in a society of amber. But the longer it got, the less unique it became. I finally wondered if the idea of unfreedom can be sustained in the mind.

MARCUS. You relied on that.

ADRIAN. Yes. But I had to keep injecting melodramatic reminders. The brain tires of unfreedom. It's like a bad back – you simply learn to avoid making certain movements . . . like . . . whatever's in this ceiling; or if nothing is; we still have to live, and talk, and the rest of it. I really thought I knew, but I saw that I didn't; it's been an education tonight. I'd love to ask you something, Marcus – why do you carry a gun?

MARCUS. I don't, normally. I was planning a trip into the mountains in Algeria – still pretty rough up there in places.

He looks at his watch.

MAYA. He fought a battle in Mexico last year. In the Chiappas. Like a cowboy.

MARCUS. Not really – no one was hurt.

ADRIAN. What the hell do you go to those places for?

MARCUS. It interests me – where there is no law, people alone with their customs. I started out to be an anthropologist.

ADRIAN. What happened?

MARCUS. The Nazis, the war. You were too young, I guess.

ADRIAN. I was in the army in the fifties, but after Korea and before Vietnam.

MARCUS. You're a lucky generation, you missed everything.

ADRIAN. I wonder sometimes. History came at us like a rumour. We were never really there.

MARCUS. Is that why you come here?

ADRIAN. Might be part of it. We're always smelling the smoke but we're never quite sure who the devil really is. Drives us nuts.

MARCUS. You don't like ambiguity.

ADRIAN. Oh sure – providing it's clear. (*He laughs.*) Or maybe it's always clearer in somebody else's country.

MARCUS. I was just about to say – the first time I came to America – a few years after the war . . .

ADRIAN. . . . . You're not an American citizen, are you?

MARCUS. Very nearly, but I had a little . . . ambiguity with your Immigration Department. (*He smiles.*)

ADRIAN. You came from the wrong country.

MARCUS. No – it was the right country when I boarded ship for New York. But the Communists took over here while I was on the high seas. A Mr Donahue, Immigration Inspector, Port of New York did not approve. He put me in a cage.

ADRIAN. Why!

MARCUS. Suspicion I was a Red agent. Actually, I'd come on an invitation to lecture at Syracuse University – I'd published my first two – or it may have been three novels in Paris by then. I phoned the university – from my cage – and they were appalled – but no one lifted a finger, of course, and I was shipped back to Europe. It was terribly unambiguous, Adrian – you were a Fascist country, to me. I was wrong, of course, but so it appeared. Anyway, I decided to come home and have a look here – I stepped off the train directly into the arms of our police.

ADRIAN. As an American spy.

MARCUS (*laughs*). What else?

ADRIAN (*nodding*). I got ya, Marcus.

MARCUS. Yes. (*Slight pause.*) But it's better now.

ADRIAN *glances at* SIGMUND.

It has been, anyway. But one has to be of the generation that can remember. Otherwise, it's as you say – a sort of rumour that has no reality – excepting for oneself.

SIGMUND *drinks deeply from his glass. Slight pause.*

ADRIAN (*stands, and from behind* SIGMUND *looks down at him for an instant*).

She's sure to come, huh?

MARCUS. I'm sure she will.

ADRIAN (*strolls to the window at Right, stretching his back and arms. He looks out of the window*). It's starting to snow. (*Slight pause.*) God, it's a beautiful city. (*He lingers there for a moment, then walks, his hands thrust into his back pockets.*) What do you suppose would happen if I went to the Minister of the Interior tonight? – If I lost my mind and knocked on his door and raised hell about this?

MARCUS *turns to him, eyebrows raised.*

I'm serious.

MARCUS. Well . . . What happened when you tried to reason with Johnson or Nixon during Vietnam?

ADRIAN. Right. But of course we could go into the streets, which you can't . . .

SIGMUND. Why not?

ADRIAN (*surprised*). With all their tanks here?

SIGMUND. Yes, even so. (*Pause.*) Is only a question of the fantasy. In this country we have not Las Vegas. The

American knows very well is almost impossible to winning money from this slot machine. But he is enjoying to experience hope. He is paying for the hope. For us, is inconceivable. Before such a machine we would experience only despair. For this reason we do not go into the street.

ADRIAN. You're more realistic about power . . .

SIGMUND. This is mistake, Adrian, we are not realistic. We also believe we can escaping power – by telling lies. For this reason, I think you have difficulty to write about us. You cannot imagine how fantastically we lie.

MARCUS. I don't think we're any worse than others . . .

SIGMUND. Oh certainly, yes – but perhaps is not exactly lying because we do not expect to deceive anyone; the professor lies to the student, the student to the professor – but each knows the other is lying. We must lie, it is our only freedom. To lie is our slot machine – we know we cannot win but it gives us the feeling of hope. Is like a serious play, which no one really believes but the technique is admirable. Our country is now a theatre, where no one is permitted to walk out, and everyone is obliged to applaud.

MARCUS. That is a marvellous description, Sigmund – of the whole world.

SIGMUND. No, I must object – when Adrian speaks to me it is always his personal opinion. But with us, is impossible to speaking so simply, we must always making theatre.

MARCUS. I've been as plain as I know how to be. What is it you don't believe?

SIGMUND (*laughs*). But that is the problem in the theatre – I believe everything but I am convinced of nothing.

MAYA. It's enough.

SIGMUND. Excuse me, Maya – for me is not enough; if I am waking up in New York one morning, I must have concrete reason, not fantastic reason.

MAYA. Darling, they've taken your book . . .

SIGMUND (*with sudden force*). But is my country – is this reason to leave my country!

MAYA. There are people who love you enough to want to keep you from prison. What is fantastic about that?

SIGMUND (*turns to* MARCUS – *with a smile*). You are loving me, Marcus?

MARCUS *overwhelmed by resentment, turns to* SIGMUND, *silent*.

Then we have not this reason. (*Slight pause.*) Therefore . . . perhaps you have come back for different reason.

MARCUS. I came back to prevent a calamity, a disaster for all of us . . .

SIGMUND. Yes, but is also for them a calamity. If I am in prison the whole world will know they are gangster. This is not intelligent – my book are published in nine country. For them is also disaster.

MARCUS. So this fellow in London? These threats? They're not serious?

SIGMUND. I am sure they wish me to believe so, therefore is very serious.

MARCUS. You don't believe a word I've told you, do you? There was no man at all in London; that conversation never happened? There'll be no arrest? No trial?

SIGMUND (*pause*). I think not.

MARCUS. Then give me back my pistol.

SIGMUND *does not move*. MARCUS *holds out his hand*.

Give it to me, you're in no danger; I've invented the whole thing.

SIGMUND *is motionless*.

Are you simply a thief? Why are you keeping it?

SIGMUND *is silent*.

MAYA. Marcus . . .

MARCUS. I insist he answer me . . . (*To* SIGMUND.) Why are you keeping that pistol? (*He laughs.*) But of course you know perfectly well I've told you the truth; it was just too good an opportunity to cover me with your contempt . . . in her eyes, (*Pointing toward* ADRIAN.) and the eyes of the world.

ADRIAN. Now, Marcus, I had no intention . . .

MARCUS. Oh come now, Adrian, he's been writing this story for you all evening! *New York Times* feature on Socialist decadence.

ADRIAN. Now wait a minute . . .

MARCUS. But it's so obvious . . . !

ADRIAN. Wait a minute, will you? He has a right to be uneasy.

MARCUS. No more than I do, and for quite the same reason.

ADRIAN. Why!

MARCUS (*laughs*). To whom am *I* talking, Adrian – the *New York Times*, or your novel, or you?

ADRIAN. For Christ's sake, are you serious?

MARCUS (*laughs*). Why not? You may turn out to be as dangerous to me as he believes I am to him. Yes!

ADRIAN *looks astonished.*

Why is it any more absurd? Especially after that last piece of yours, which you'll pardon me, was stuffed with the most primitive misunderstandings of what it means to live in this country. You haven't a clue, Adrian – you'll forgive me, but I have to say that. So I'm entitled to a bit of uneasiness.

ADRIAN. Marcus, are you asking me to account for myself?

MARCUS. By no means, but why must I?

MAYA. Why don't we all go to the playground and swing with the other children?

MARCUS (*laughs*). Very good, yes.

MAYA (*to* ADRIAN). Why is he so complicated? They allow him this house to store his father's library. These books earn hard currency. To sell them he must have a passport.

MARCUS. Oh, he knows all that, dear – it's hopeless; when did the facts ever change a conviction? It doesn't matter. (*He looks at his watch.*)

ADRIAN. It does, though. It's a terrible thing. It's maddening.

MARCUS (*denigrating*). Well . . .

ADRIAN. It is, you know it is. Christ, you're such old friends, you're writers . . . I never understood the sadness in this country, but I swear, I think it's . . .

MARCUS. Oh, come off it, Adrian – what country isn't sad?

ADRIAN. I think you've accepted something.

MARCUS. And you haven't?

ADRIAN. Goddammit, Marcus, we can still speak for ourselves! And not for some . . . (*He breaks off.*)

MARCUS. Some what?

ADRIAN (*walks away*). . . . . Well, never mind.

MARCUS. I've spoken for no one but myself here, Adrian. If there seems to be some . . . unspoken interest . . . well, there is, of course. I am interested in seeing that this country does not fall back into darkness. And if he must sacrifice something for that, I think he should. That's plain enough, isn't it?

ADRIAN. I guess the question is . . . how you feel about that yourself.

MARCUS (*laughs*). But I feel terribly about it. I think it's dreadful. I think there's no question he is our best living writer. Must I go on, or is that enough?
Silence.

What change can feelings make? It is a situation which I can tell you – *no one wants* . . . no one. If I flew into an orgasm of self-revelation here it might seem more candid, but it would change nothing . . . (except possibly to multiply the confusion).

MAYA (*to* ADRIAN). I think you were saying the same thing

before . . . Tell him.

MARCUS. What?

ADRIAN. Whether it matters anymore, what anyone feels . . . about anything. Whether we're not just some sort of . . . filament that only lights up when it's plugged into whatever power there is.

MAYA. It's interesting.

MARCUS. I don't know – it seems rather childish. When was a man ever conceivable apart from society? Unless you're looking for the angel who wrote each of our blessed names in his book of gold. The collective giveth and the collective taketh away – beyond that . . .

He looks to the ceiling.

was never anything but a sentimental metaphor; a god which now is simply a form of art. Whose style may still move us, but there was never any mercy in that plaster. The only difference now, it seems to me, is that we've ceased to expect any.

ADRIAN. I know one reason I came. I know it's an awkward question, but – those tanks bivouacked out there in the countryside . . . do they figure at all in your minds?

MAYA. Do you write *every minute*?

ADRIAN. Well, do they? (*To* MARCUS.) Are they part of your lives at all?

MARCUS. I don't really know . . .

ADRIAN. Maya? It interests me.

MAYA. It's such a long time, now. And you don't see them unless you drive out there . . .

MARCUS. It's hard to say.

ADRIAN (*of* SIGMUND). Why do you suppose he can't stop thinking about them? I bet there isn't an hour a day when they don't cross his mind.

MAYA. Because he is a genius. When he enters the tram the conductor refuses to accept his fare. In the grocery store they give him the best oranges. The usher bows in the theatre when she shows him to his seat.

She goes to SIGMUND, *touches his hair.*

He is our Sigmund. He is loved, he creates our memories. Therefore, it is only a question of time when he will create the departure of these tanks, and they will go home. And then we shall all be ourselves, with nothing overhead but the sky, and he will turn into a monument standing in the park.

Her eyes fill with tears, she turns up his face.

Go, darling. Please. There is nothing left for you.

SIGMUND (*touches her face*). Something, perhaps. We shall see.

MAYA *moves Right to the window, sips a drink.*

IRINA (*with a swimming gesture to* MARCUS). I am bathing?

MARCUS. Yes, of course – come, I'll get you a towel. (*He starts to rise.*)

MAYA (*looking out of the window*). She'd better wait a little – I used all the hot water. (*With a laugh, to* SIGMUND.) I came tonight to take a bath!

MARCUS *laughs.*

ADRIAN. Marcus, when they arrested you . . .

MAYA (*suddenly*). Will you stop writing, for Christ's sake! Isn't there something else to talk about?

MARCUS. Why not? – if he's interested?

MAYA. Are we some sick fish in a tank! (*To* ADRIAN.) Stop it! (*She get up, goes to the drink table.*) What the hell do you expect people to *do*? What *is* it?

MARCUS. You've had enough, dear . . .

MAYA (*pouring*). I have not had enough, dear. (*She suddenly slams the glass down on the table.*) Fuck all this diplomacy! (*At* ADRIAN.) You're in no position to judge anybody! We have nothing to be ashamed of!

MARCUS (*turning away in disgust*). Oh for God's sake . . .

MAYA. You know what he brought when he came to me? A bottle of milk!

Perplexed, MARCUS *turns to her.*

I wake up and he's in the kitchen, drinking *milk*!

She waits before MARCUS, *awaiting his reaction.*

A grown man!

MARCUS (*to calm her*). Well, they drink a lot of it in the States.

MAYA (*quietly, seeking to explain*). He smelled like a baby, all night.

MARCUS (*stands*). I'll make you some coffee . . .

He starts past her, but she stops him with her hand on his arm, frightened and remorseful. She kisses him.

MAYA. I'm going home. (*She takes his hand, tries to lead him toward* SIGMUND *with imperative force.*) Come, be his friend . . . you are friends, darling . . .

The telephone in the bedroom rings. She turns up to the entrance in surprise.

Goddamn that Hilton!

She starts towards the bedroom, but as the telephone rings again, MARCUS *goes up and exits into the bedroom. She comes to* SIGMUND.

Darling . . . (*She points up to the ceiling – speaking softly in desperation.*) I really don't think there is anything there. I would never do that to you, you know that. I think it was only to make himself interesting – he can't write anymore; it left him . . . (*In anguish.*) . . . it left him!

SIGMUND. I know.

MAYA. He loves you, he loves you, darling . . . ! (*Gripping her head.*) My God, I'm sick . . .

She starts upstage as MARCUS *enters. He has a stunned look. She halts, seeing him, looks at him questioningly.* SIGMUND *turns to look at him, and* ADRIAN. *After a moment . . .*

MARCUS (*turning to* SIGMUND *with a gesture inviting him to go* to the phone.

It's Alexandra.

SIGMUND *does not move.*

. . . she wishes to speak to you.

SIGMUND *stands, confounded by* MARCUS's *look, and goes out into the bedroom.* MARCUS *remains there, staring.*

MAYA. What?

MARCUS *is silent, staring.*

ADRIAN. Something happen?

MARCUS *crosses the stage and descends into his chair, his face transfixed by some enigma.*

MAYA (*in fright . . . starting up toward the bedroom.*) Sigmund . . . !

SIGMUND *enters, halts, shakes his head uttering an almost soundless laugh, his eyes alive to something incredible.*

MARCUS. They're returning his manuscript.

MAYA *claps her hands together, then crosses herself, her face between explosive joy and some terror, rigid, sobered.*

ADRIAN (*grabs* SIGMUND *by the shoulders*). Is it true?

MARCUS. She may be able to bring it when she comes.

ADRIAN. Sigmund!

He kisses him. They look at each other and laugh.

SIGMUND (*half-smiling*). You believe it?

ADRIAN (*takes aback*). Don't you?

SIGMUND (*laughs*). I don't know! (*He walks, dumbfounded.*) . . . Yes, I suppose I believe. (*He suddenly laughs.*) Why not! They have made me ridiculous, therefore I must believe it.

MARCUS. Well, the main thing is, you . . .

SIGMUND. Yes, that is the main thing. I must call Elizabeth . . .(*He starts to the bedroom, but looks at his watch.*) No . . . she will not yet be home.

ADRIAN (*to all*). What could it mean? (*He laughs, seeing* SIGMUND.) You look punchy. (*He grabs him.*) Wake up! –

you got it back! . . . Listen, come to Paris with me . . .
with the boy and Elizabeth. We'll get you a visa – you can
be in New York in ten days. We'll go to my publisher, I'll
break his arm, we'll get you a tremendous advance and
you're on your way.

SIGMUND (*laughing*). Wait, wait . . .

ADRIAN. Say yes! Come on! You can waste the rest of your
life in this goddamned country. Jesus, why can't they steal
it again tomorrow? – (*To the ceiling:*) I didn't mean that
about the country. But it's infuriating – they play you like
a yo-yo.

SIGMUND (*sits; an aura of irony on his voice*). So, Maya . . .
you are immortal again.

ADRIAN. Is *she* that character?

MAYA. Of course.

ADRIAN. She sounded terrific.

MAYA. She is the best woman he has ever written – fantastic,
complicated personality. (*To* SIGMUND.) What is there to
keep you now? It is enough, no?

IRINA. Is good?

MARCUS (*patting her*). Yes, very good.

SIGMUND. She is so lucky – she understands nothing. We
also understand nothing – but for us is not lucky.

MAYA. We should go to Francesco's later – we should have
a party.

SIGMUND (*turns to her with a faint smile*). It is strange, eh?
We have such good news and we are sad.

MARCUS. It isn't sadness.

SIGMUND. Perhaps only some sort of humiliation. (*He shakes
his head.*) We must admire them – they are very intelligent
– they can even create unhappiness with good news.

ADRIAN (*to* MARCUS). What do you suppose happened?

MARCUS. I've no idea.

ADRIAN. It seems like a gesture of some kind. Is it?

MARCUS. I haven't the foggiest.

ADRIAN. Could it be that I was here?

MARCUS. Who knows? Of course they would like to make peace with him, it's a gesture in that sense.

SIGMUND *looks across at him.*

I think you ought to consider it that way.

SIGMUND. It is their contempt; they are laughing.

MARCUS. Not necessarily – Some of them have great respect for you.

SIGMUND. No-no, they are laughing.

MAYA. Why are you such children?

SIGMUND *turns to her.*

It is not respect and it is not contempt – it is nothing.

ADRIAN. But it must mean something.

MAYA. Why? They have the power to take it and the power to give it back.

ADRIAN. Well that's a meaning.

MAYA. You didn't know that before? When it rains you get wet – that is not exactly meaningful. (*To the three.*) There's nothing to say; it is a terrible embarrassment for geniuses but there is simply no possible comment to be made.

SIGMUND. How is in Shakespeare? – 'We are like flies to little boys, they kill us for their sport.'

MAYA. They are not killing you at all. Not at all.

SIGMUND. Why are you angry with me? I am not obliged to ask why something happens?

MAYA. Because you can live happily and you don't want to.

ADRIAN. It's not so simple.

MAYA. But for you it is! You are so rich, Adrian, you live so well – why must he be heroic?

ADRIAN. I've never told him to . . .

MAYA. Then tell him to get out! Be simple, be clear to him . . .

ADRIAN. I've been very clear to him . . .

MAYA. Good! (*To* SIGMUND.) So the three of us are of the same opinion, you see? Let's have a party at Francesco's ... call Elizabeth ... a farewell party. All right?

He looks up at her.

It is all finished, darling!

He smiles, shaking his head. She is frightened and angry.

What? What is it? What more can be said?

SIGMUND (*with a certain laughter*). Is like some sort of theatre, no? Very bad theatre – our emotions have no connection with the event. Myself also – I *must* speak, darling – I do not understand myself. I must confess, I have feeling of gratitude; *before* they have stolen my book I was never grateful. *Now* I am grateful – (*His laughter vanishes.*) I cannot accept such confusion, Maya, is very bad for my mentality. I must speak! I think we must all speak now!

He ends looking at MARCUS; *his anger is open.*

MARCUS. What can I tell you? I know nothing.

SIGMUND. I am sure not, but we can speculate, perhaps? (*To* MAYA.) Please, darling – sit; we must wait for Alexandra, we have nothing to do. Please, Adrian – sit down . . . I have some idea . . .

ADRIAN *sits.* SIGMUND *continues to* MAYA.

. . . which I would like to discuss before I leave my country.

MAYA *sits slowly, apprehensively. He turns to* MARCUS, *adopting a quiet, calm air.*

Is possible, Marcus – there was some sort of mistake? Perhaps only one police commander has made this decision for himself – to stealing my book? Perhaps the government was also surprised?

MARCUS *considers in silence.*

SIGMUND. I am interested your opinion. *I* think so, perhaps – no?

MARCUS. Do you know if they were the Security Police?

SIGMUND. Yes, Security Police.

MARCUS. *They* might, I suppose.

SIGMUND. I think so. But in this case . . . this fellow in London taxi – is possible he was also speaking for himself?

MARCUS. I can't believe that.

SIGMUND. But if he was speaking for government . . . such terrible thing against me – why have they chosen to re-turning my manuscript? I think is not logical, no?

MARCUS. . . . Unless they had second thoughts, and felt it would make it easier for you to leave.

SIGMUND. Yes. That is very strong idea.

ADRIAN. I think that's it.

SIGMUND. Very good, yes. But at same time, if have manu-script – you do not object that I . . . ?

MARCUS. Go ahead – it's simply that I know no more than . . .

SIGMUND. You understand is very important to me . . . I must understand why I am leaving.

MARCUS. Of course. Go ahead.

SIGMUND (*slight pause*). If I have manuscript, I must proba-bly conclude is *not* dangerous for me here, no? I must be-lieve is only some particular antagonistic enemy who wish me to go out. Is possible?

MARCUS. What can I tell you?

SIGMUND (*with nearly an outcry through his furious control*). But you know you are sad! I am sad, Maya is sad – if was some sort of mistake . . . why we are not happy?
MAYA *gets up and strides towards the bedroom.*
Maya?

MAYA (*hardly turning back*). I'm going home . . .

SIGMUND (*leaps up and intercepts her*). No-no, – we must have celebration! (*He grips her hands.*)

MAYA. Let me go!

SIGMUND. No! We have tremendous good news, we must

have correct emotion!

MAYA (*wrenching her hands free, pointing at his pocket*). Give me that thing. . . . Give it to me!

SIGMUND. My God – I had forgotten it. (*He takes out the pistol, looks at it.*)

MAYA. Please. Sigmund. Please . . . !

SIGMUND. I have crazy idea . . .

MAYA (*weeping*). Sigmund . . .

SIGMUND (*moving toward the piano*). One time very long ago, I have read in American detective story . . . that criminal has placed revolver inside piano.

He sets the pistol on the strings, and comes around to the bench. Then someone is playing very fortissimo . . . something like Beethoven . . . (*Raising his hands over the keyboard.*) . . . and he is firing the pistol.

ADRIAN. What the hell are you doing?

SIGMUND (*smashes his hands down on the keyboard*). Ha! Is not true.

ADRIAN (*stands*). What the hell are you doing?

SIGMUND. Wait! I have idea . . . (*He reaches over, takes out the pistol and cocks it.*)

MAYA. Marcus!

SIGMUND (*replacing the cocked pistol in the piano*). Now we shall see . . .

ADRIAN (*rushing MAYA away from the piano*). Watch out!

SIGMUND (*crashes his hands down – the gun explodes, the strings reverberating.*) Is true! (*Reaching in and taking out the revolver.*) My God, I am so happy . . . (*Holding up the revolver.*) The truth is alive in our country, Marcus!

He comes and sits near MARCUS.

Is unmistakable, no? – when something is true?

He looks at the pistol, puts it in his pocket. MARCUS turns to him only now. MAYA suddenly weeps, sobbing, and makes for the bedroom.

I cannot permit you to leave, Maya! (*She halts, turning to him in terror.*)

I must insist, darling – is most important evening of my life and I understand nothing. Why do you weep, why do you go? If I am ridiculous I must understand why! Please . . . sit. Perhaps you can say something.

She sits, a distance from him and MARCUS. ADRIAN *remains standing, catching his breath; he leans his head on his hand, as though caught by a rush of sadness and he shakes his head incredulously, glancing at* MARCUS.

MARCUS. What is it? What *is* it!

SIGMUND. This fellow . . . this fellow in taxi who has threatened me – what was his name?

MARCUS. I don't recall, I only heard it once. Granitz, I think. Or Grodnitz. But I'm sure he didn't know you.

SIGMUND. Grodnitz.

MARCUS. . . . Or Granitz.

ADRIAN. You know him?

SIGMUND. . . . No. (*Slight pause.*) No Granitz. No Grodnitz. (*Slight pause. He takes the pistol out of his pocket, looks at it in his hand, then turns again to* MARCUS.)

He exists? Or is imaginary man?

MARCUS *is silent.*

Was *ever* discussion of trial for me? Or is imaginary trial?

MARCUS *is silent.* SIGMUND *looks at the pistol again, then stretching over to* MARCUS *he places it in his hand.*

I believe I have no danger, at the moment.

Slight pause. A long pause. No one dares do more than glance at MARCUS *whose face is filled with his fury. The pause lengthens.* SIGMUND *looks at his watch.*

I will try to call Elizabeth.

MARCUS. The sole function of every other writer is to wish he were you.

SIGMUND *stands, looks to* MAYA, *who avoids his eyes. He*

exits into the bedroom. After a moment . . .

ADRIAN (*sotto, to assuage* MARCUS). He's terribly scared
. . .

MARCUS (*slight pause. Like a final verdict*). I couldn't care
less. (*He looks at his watch.*)

ADRIAN (*silent for a moment*). For what it's worth . . . I know
he has tremendous feeling for you.

MARCUS. For his monument. To build his monument he has
to prove that everyone else is a coward or corrupt. My mistake was to offer him my help – it's a menace to his lonely
grandeur. No one is permitted anything but selfishness.
He's insane.

ADRIAN. Oh come on . . .

MARCUS. He's paranoid – these letters to the foreign press
are for nothing but to bring on another confrontation – it
was too peaceful; they were threatening him with toler-
ance. He must find evil or he can't be good.

MAYA. Let's not talk about it anymore . . .

MARCUS. I exist too, Maya! I am not dancing around that
megalomania again. (*Slight pause.*)

ADRIAN. I can't blame you, but I wish you wouldn't cut out
on him yet. Look, I'll stay through the week, maybe I can
convince him. Does he have a week?

MARCUS (*slowly turns to* ADRIAN). How would I know?

ADRIAN. All I meant was whether you . . .

MARCUS. I won't have anymore of this, Adrian!
Slight pause.

ADRIAN. I believe you – I've told him to get out.

MARCUS. No you haven't; you've insinuated.

ADRIAN. Christ's sake, you've heard me say . . .

MARCUS. I *have* heard you.
They are facing each other. Slight pause.
You don't believe me, Adrian . . . not really.
ADRIAN *can't answer.*

MARCUS. So it's all over. It's the end of him. – I've been there. He will smash his head against the walls, and the rest of us will pay for his grandeur.

Slight pause. ADRIAN *turns front in his conflict.* SIGMUND *enters.* MARCUS *turns away.*

MAYA (*with a tonal attempt at cheerfulness*). Did you reach her? Elizabeth?

SIGMUND. She is very happy. (*To* MARCUS.) She send you her greetings – she is grateful.

Slight pause.

I also.

MARCUS *half-turns toward him.* SIGMUND *says no more, goes to his chair and sits.*

ADRIAN. Sigmund? (SIGMUND *glances at him.*) Do you trust me?

SIGMUND *is silent.*

I'm convinced he's told you the truth.

SIGMUND *is silent.*

In all the times we've talked about you, he's never shown anything but a wide-open pride in you, and your work. He's with you. You have to believe that.

SIGMUND *turns, stares at* MARCUS's *profile for a moment. Then looks at* MAYA. *She ultimately turns slightly away. He looks down at the floor.*

SIGMUND. I am afraid; that is all. I think I will not be able to write in some other country.

ADRIAN. Oh, that's impossible . . .

SIGMUND. I am not cosmopolitan writer, I am provincial writer. I believe I must hear my language every day, I must walk in these particular streets. I think in New York I will have only some terrible silence. Is like old tree – it is difficult to moving old tree, they most probably die.

ADRIAN. But if they lock you up . . .

SIGMUND. Yes, but that is my fate; I must accept my fate.

But to run away because of some sort of rumour – I have only some rumour, no? How will I support this silence that I have brought on myself? This is terrible idea, no? How I can accept to be so ridiculous? Therefore, is reasonable, I believe – that I must absolutely understand who is speaking to me.

ADRIAN (*slight pause, a hesitation*). I'm going to level with you, Sigmund – I think you're being far too . . .

SIGMUND (*a frustrated outburst*). I am not crazy, Adrian!

All turn to him, fear in their faces. He spreads his arms, with an upward glance.

Who is commanding me? Who is this voice? *Who is speaking to me?*

MAYA. They.

An instant's silence; she seems ashamed to look directly at SIGMUND. *She gestures almost imperceptibly upward.*

It is there.

MARCUS (*in protest*). Maya!

MAYA. Why not! (*To* SIGMUND). They have heard it all.

MARCUS (*to* SIGMUND *and* ADRIAN). It isn't true, there's nothing.

MAYA (*persisting, to* SIGMUND). He has risked everything . . . for you. God knows what will happen for what has been said here.

MARCUS (*to* SIGMUND). There's nothing . . . she can't know . . . (*To* MAYA.) You can't know that . . .

MAYA (*her eyes to the ceiling*). Who else have we been speaking to all evening! (*To them all.*) Who does not believe it? (*To* MARCUS.) It is his life, darling – we must begin to say what we believe. Somewhere, we must begin!

Pause. She sits a distance from SIGMUND; *only after a moment does she turn to face him as she fights down her shame and her fear of him.*

SIGMUND. So.

MAYA (*downing her shame*). Just so, yes. You must go.

SIGMUND. For your sake.

MAYA. Yes.

MARCUS (*softly, facing front*). It isn't true.

MAYA. And yours. For all of us.

SIGMUND. You must . . . deliver me? My departure?

    MAYA *stiffens. She cannot speak.*

SIGMUND. For your programme? His passport . . . ?

ADRIAN. Sigmund, it's enough . . .

MAYA. He had no need to return, except he loves you. There was no need. That is also true.

SIGMUND (*his head clamped in his hands*). My God . . . Maya. *Pause.*

    (*To* MARCUS.) They brought you back to make sure my departure?

ADRIAN (*aborting the violence coming*). Come on, Sigmund, it's enough . . .

SIGMUND (*trying to laugh*). But she is not some sort of whore! I have many years with this woman . . . !

ADRIAN. What more do you *want*!

MARCUS. Her humiliation; she's not yet on her knees to him. We are now to take our places, you see, at the foot of the cross, as he floats upward through the plaster on the wings of his immortal contempt. We lack remorse, it spoils the picture.

    He glares, smiling at SIGMUND *who seems on the verge of springing at him.*

ADRIAN (*to* SIGMUND). Forget it, Sigmund – come on . . .

    (*To* MARCUS.) Maybe you ought to call that Alexandra woman.

MARCUS. She'll be along.

    Silence. The moment expands. SIGMUND *stares front, gripping his lower face.* ADRIAN *is glancing at him with apprehension.* MAYA *is looking at no one.*

SIGMUND (*to* MAYA). You can say nothing to me?

MAYA (*slight pause*). You know my feeling.

SIGMUND. I, not. I know your name. Who is this woman?

MARCUS. Don't play that game with him.

SIGMUND. It is a game?

ADRIAN. Come on, fellas . . .

SIGMUND (*irritated, to* ADRIAN). Is interesting to me. (*To* MARCUS.) What is your game? What did you mean?

MARCUS. It's called Power. Or Moral Monopoly. The winner takes all the justifications. When you write this, Adrian, I hope you include the fact that they refused him a visa for many years and he was terribly indignant – the right to leave was sacred to civilisation. Now he has that right and it's an insult. You can draw your own conclusions.

SIGMUND. And what is the conclusion?

MARCUS. You are a moral blackmailer. We have all humoured you, Sigmund, out of some misplaced sense of responsibility to our literature. Or maybe it's only our terror of vanishing altogether. We aren't the Russians – after you and Otto and Peter there aren't a handful to keep the breath of life in this language. We have taken all the responsibility and left you all the freedom to call us morally bankrupt. But now you're free to go, so the responsibility moves to you. Now it's yours. All yours. We have done what was possible; now you will do what is necessary, or turn out our lights. And that is where it stands.

SIGMUND (*slight pause*). This is all?

MARCUS *is silent*.

ADRIAN. What more can be said, Sigmund? What can they give you? It's pointless.

SIGMUND (*turns to* MAYA). What you can give me, Maya? (*She is silent.*) There is nothing? I am only some sort of . . . comical Jesus Christ? Is only my egotism? This is all?

In silence, MAYA *turns to face him.*

You understand what I ask you?

MAYA. Yes.

SIGMUND. You cannot? (*Slight pause. Then he glances toward* MARCUS.) After so many years . . . so many conversations . . . so many hope and disaster – you can only speak for them?

He gestures toward the ceiling.

Is terrible, no? Why we have lived?

ADRIAN (*to cut off his mounting anger*). Sigmund . . .

SIGMUND (*swiftly, his eyes blazing*). Why have you come here? What do you want in this country?

ADRIAN (*astonished*). What the hell are you . . . ?

SIGMUND. You are scientist observing the specimens – this whore? This clever fellow making business with these gangsters?

ADRIAN. For Christ's sake, Sigmund, what can I do!

SIGMUND. They are killing us, Adrian – they have destroyed my friends! You are free man, (*With a gesture toward the ceiling.*) why you are obliged to be clever? – Why do you come here, Adrian?

MAYA. To save his book.

ADRIAN. That's a lie!

MAYA. But it's exactly what you told me an hour ago. (*She stands, and to both* SIGMUND *and* ADRIAN.) What is the sin? He has come for his profit, to rescue two years' work, to make more money . . .

ADRIAN. That's a goddamned lie!

MAYA. And for friendship! Oh yes – his love for you. I believe it! Like ours. Absolutely like ours! Is love not love because there is some profit in it? Who speaks only for his heart? And yes, I speak to them now – this moment, this very moment to them, that they may have mercy on my programme, on his passport. Always to them, in some part to them for my profit – here and everywhere in this world! Just as you do.

SIGMUND. I speak for Sigmund.

MAYA. Only Sigmund? Then why can't you speak for Sigmund in America? Because you will not have them in America to hate! And if you cannot hate you cannot write and you will not be Sigmund anymore, but another lousy refugee ordering his chicken soup in broken English – and where is the profit in that? They are your theme, your life, your partner in this dance that cannot stop, or you will die of silence! (*She moves toward him . . . and tenderly.*) They are in you, darling. And if you stay . . . it is also for your profit . . . as it is for ours to tell you to go. Who can speak for himself alone?

A heavy brass knocker is heard from below.

SIGMUND *lifts his eyes to the ceiling.*

MARCUS *stands, faces* SIGMUND *who now turns to him. Silence.*

SIGMUND. Tell her, please . . . is impossible . . . any transaction. Only to return my property.

MAYA (*with an abjectness, a terror, taking his hand and kissing it*). Darling . . . For my sake. For this little life that I have made . . .

MARCUS (*with anger, disgust*). Stop it! (*He turns to* SIGMUND.) For your monument. For the bowing ushers in the theatre. For the power . . . the power to bring down everyone.

SIGMUND (*spreads his hands, looks up at the ceiling*). I don't know. (*He turns to* MARCUS.) But I will never leave. Never.

Another knock is heard. MARCUS, *his face set, goes out and up the corridor.* SIGMUND *turns to* MAYA. *She walks away, her face expressionless, and stands at the window staring out.*

Forgive me, Maya.

She doesn't turn to him. He looks to ADRIAN.

Is quite simple. We are ridiculous people now. And when we try to escape it, we are ridiculous too.

ADRIAN. No.

SIGMUND. I think so. But we cannot help ourselves. I must give you . . . certain letters, I wish to keep them . . . before you leave. (*Sitting.*) I have one some years ago from Malraux. Very elegant. *French,* you know? Also Julia Ilyesh, Hungarian . . . very wise fellow. Heinrich Böll, Germany, one letter. Kobo Abe, Japan – he also. Saul Bellow. Also Cortazar, Brazil . . .

Slight pause.

My God, eh? So many writers! Like snow . . . like forest . . . these enormous trees everywhere on the earth. Marvellous.

Slight pause. A welling up in him. He suddenly cries out to MAYA *across the stage.*

Maya! Forgive me . . .

He hurries to her.

I cannot help it.

MAYA. I know. (*She turns to him, reaches out and touches his face.*) Thank you.

SIGMUND (*surprised, he is motionless for an instant, then pulls her into his arms, and holding her face*). Oh, my God! Thank you, Maya.

The voices of MARCUS *and* ALEXANDRA *are heard approaching from the darkness up the corridor. The three of them turn toward the door.*

IRINA (*revolving her finger, to* MAYA). Now, music?

Curtain.

Afterword

When the ballroom of the Mayflower Hotel on Connecticut Avenue, Washington, was redecorated in 1983 the painters and plasterers found twenty-eight hidden microphones. The Mayflower, for long popular with politicians, diplomats and businessmen, had been turned into a kind of permanent theatre by the FBI, or whatever other agency was interested in the alchemical transformation of knowledge into power. Scarcely a shock in a country which had experienced the cynical corruptions of Watergate, it was nonetheless a reminder of the fragile and suspect nature of the real. Those who had once been dismissed as hopelessly paranoid could now claim to have been the most rational of social analysts, for the politicians and their agents had seemingly conspired to corrupt not only the political process but also our sense of reality. When the insane run the asylum who can we trust to define the nature of sanity?

The Archbishop's Ceiling is set in eastern Europe but the pressure of a quarter of a century of illegal surveillance at home can be felt behind what appears at first to be a political drama in which one man, a writer called Sigmund, comes to embody a sense of resistance to the apparatus of the state. At a time when power asserts its presumptive rights he chooses to stay and fight when he could leave – indeed when his exile is the price of his survival as an artist. But, like much else in the play, this is misleading. What appears to be a purely political play slowly reveals itself as a study of metaphysics, a debate about the nature of reality and the problematic status of morality in a world whose certainties dissolve so easily into mere performance.

A group of people assemble in the down-at-heel splendour of a one-time Archbishop's palace: Adrian is an American novelist whose reasons for travelling east are deeply ambiguous; Maya, a one-time poet and actress, who, like her companion, Marcus – also a novelist – may or may not be in league with the authorities. These are joined by Sigmund, a dissident novelist, under pressure to leave for the West. They meet in the conviction – never fully confirmed – that they are overheard by microphones concealed in the room's ornate ceiling. In other words they are turned into actors and their lives into theatre; but there is, finally, no evidence for the existence of the audience before whom they take themselves to be performing. There is no stable reality. They exist in a factitious world. And just as they inhabit the fictions of the state so they, as writers, counter with their own fictions. But in an existence in which performance becomes a personal and political necessity how can morality be constructed? And beyond the psychological, social and political questions which the play raises is a metaphysical anxiety. The Archbishop's palace has fallen into disuse as a religious building. The baroque decorations are now lost in the gloom. Where once human life was charged with significance by the conviction that we acted out our dramas in the eye of God, for whom all actions had meaning and every gesture was a cipher to be decided in terms of grace or damnation, now the suspicion is that He has withdrawn. The eye that saw, the ears that heard are now no longer there.

But there is a paradox – no less on the political than the metaphysical plane – for to believe that there is a hidden audience may be to be turned into an actor but to doubt that presence is in some way to be drained of significance, no matter how arbitrary that significance may be. To be bugged is to be violated but it is also to have one's existence confirmed and one's meaning attested. Willing submission to invisible powers is understandable even if it threatens our identity for the alternative is not only freedom but abandonment. And what meaning can we ascribe to a freedom which is exercised out of the sight of man and god? A courageous act publicly performed perhaps requires rather less courage than one done in a privacy which drains it of its social meaning. The empty auditorium has terrors scarcely less affecting than one filled with those who judge as well as observe.

Taken together, *The Archbishop's Ceiling* and his two one act plays, *Some Kind of Love Story* and *Elegy for a Lady* (published by Methuen under the composite title *Two Way Mirror*) constitute a major new phase in the career of America's leading playwright. But the break is not as radical as it may appear. In fact, behind the moral concerns, the social and political urgencies of his earlier work, there was always a fascination with the problematic status of the real. He argued for what seemed to be the manifest values of a classic American liberalism and a native existentialism in a world in which those principles were under extreme pressure. The myth of independence remained as did the language of social responsibility and the assertion of a cohesive national purpose, but the reality was otherwise. It was not merely that liberal values had deferred to a new materialism, that the independent spirit was threatened by the physical conditions and social coercions of modern American society, but that public myths now exerted an authority which threatened the individual at his or her core. Thus, in *Death of a Salesman*, Willy Loman is finally unable to separate reality from appearance. He is an actor incapable of distinguishing identity from role. As Miller said, he believed that the stars projected on the clouds from the rooftops were real stars. *The Crucible*, in turn, is at base a debate about the nature of the real and about those who claim the right to define it as much as it is a drama of moral responsibility. In *After the Fall, Incident at Vichy* and *Playing for Time* Miller tried to understand and analyse the terrible fictions of the Third Reich which quite literally rendered down the grace and complexity of the human sensibility. Thus his present concern with life as theatre, with the coercive power of private and public fictions, with the nature of the real and with the necessity to reconstruct a moral world in the ethical void left by the death of God – or those gods we have invented in order to give ourselves significance – is a natural extension of his earlier plays. But the urgency is now more apparent, the dislocations more threatening, the mood more apocalyptic, the moral certainties under greater pressure.

And if, finally, we do inhabit a world of competing fictions in which our central task is perhaps no longer to learn to distinguish the true from the false but to generate fictions which assert rather than deny human values then the role of the artist becomes central. In a sense we all summon the world into existence and coerce others onto a stage which we have set. This is the tension behind personal relationships. Projected onto a national scale this becomes potentially more lethal. The writer thus seeks to intervene but can only do so on the level of the imagination – an imagination for which the world is so much raw material, his *mise en scène*. The necessity to do so remains but it must be an inherently ambiguous enterprise, touched with guilt and characterised by a profound anxiety.

The American writer, Adrian, who comes to the Archbishop's palace does so less out of feelings of solidarity than because he seeks absolution, for the fact is that he has included Maya as a character in his fiction (she is to be a character in his new novel) just as the state tries to incorporate the individual into its fictions. The play is thus in a sense a contemplation of the ethics of writing no less than a consideration of the morality of social being. Marcus seems the writer turned betrayer, a mere apparatchik. And yet, in the Archbishop's palace, there are no certainties; there is no touchstone of veracity, no proof of sincerity and authenticity. Indeed that is the essence of the play. But the need to make some moral stand survives, the compulsion to assert the significance of identity and to acknowledge a responsibility beyond the self. How that is to be achieved in a world of fictions, in which action is turned into theatre and ethics into aesthetics, is only one of the questions posed by this complex but moving play.

CHRISTOPHER BIGSBY

Methuen's Modern Plays

Jean Anouilh	*Antigone*
	Becket
	The Lark
John Arden	*Serjeant Musgrave's Dance*
	The Workhouse Donkey
	Armstrong's Last Goodnight
John Arden and	*The Business of Good Government*
Margaretta D'Arcy	*The Royal Pardon*
	The Hero Rises Up
	The Island of the Mighty
	Vandaleur's Folly
Wolfgang Bauer	*Shakespeare the Sadist*
Rainer Werner	
Fassbinder	*Bremen Coffee*
Peter Handke	*My Foot My Tutor*
Frank Xaver Kroetz	*Stallerhof*
Brendan Behan	*The Quare Fellow*
	The Hostage
	Richard's Cork Leg
Edward Bond	*A-A-America!* and *Stone*
	Saved
	Narrow Road to the Deep North
	The Pope's Wedding
	Lear
	The Sea
	Bingo
	The Fool and *We Come to the River*
	Theatre Poems and Songs
	The Bundle
	The Woman
	The Worlds with *The Activists Papers*
	Restoration and *The Cat*
	Summer and *Fables*
Bertolt Brecht	*Mother Courage and Her Children*
	The Caucasian Chalk Circle
	The Good Person of Szechwan
	The Life of Galileo

C.P. Taylor	*And a Nightingale Sang . . .*
	Good
Peter Whelan	*The Accrington Pals*
Nigel Williams	*Line 'Em*
	Class Enemy
Charles Wood	*Veterans*
Theatre Workshop	*Oh What a Lovely War!*
Various authors	*Best Radio Plays of 1978* (Don Haworth: *Episode on a Thursday Evening:* Tom Mallin: *Halt! Who Goes There?;* Jennifer Phillips: *Daughters of Men;* Fay Weldon: *Polaris;* Jill Hyem: *Remember Me;* Richard Harris: *Is It Something I Said?*)
	Best Radio Plays of 1979 (Shirley Gee: *Typhoid Mary;* Carey Harrison: *I Never Killed My German;* Barrie Keeffe: *Heaven Scent;* John Kirkmorris: *Coxcombe;* John Peacock: *Attard in Retirement;* Olwen Wymark: *The Child*)
	Best Radio Plays of 1982 (Rhys Adrian:*Watching the Plays Together;* John Arden: *The Old Man Sleeps Alone;* Harry Barton: *Hoopoe Day;* Donald Chapman: *Invisible Writing;* Tom Stoppard: *The Dog It Was That Died;* William Trevor: *Autumn Sunshine*)

The Master Playwrights

Collections of plays by the best-known modern playwrights in value-for-money paperbacks.

John Arden	PLAYS: ONE *Serjeant Musgrave's Dance, The Workhouse Donkey, Armstrong's Last Goodnight*
Brendan Behan	THE COMPLETE PLAYS *The Hostage, The Quare Fellow, Richard's Cork Leg, Moving Out, A Garden Party, The Big House*
Edward Bond	PLAYS: ONE *Saved, Early Morning, The Pope's Wedding* PLAYS: TWO *Lear, The Sea, Narrow Road to the Deep North, Black Mass, Passion*
Noël Coward	PLAYS: ONE *Hay Fever, The Vortex, Fallen Angels, Easy Virtue* PLAYS: TWO *Private Lives, Bitter Sweet, The Marquise, Post-Mortem* PLAYS: THREE *Design for Living, Cavalcade, Conversation Piece,* and *Hands Across the Sea, Still Life* and *Fumed Oak* from *Tonight at 8.30* PLAYS: FOUR *Blithe Spirit, This Happy Breed, Present Laughter* and *Ways and Means, The Astonished Heart* and *Red Peppers* from *Tonight at 8.30* PLAYS: FIVE *Relative Values, Look After Lulu, Waiting in the Wings, Suite in Three Keys*
John Galsworthy	FIVE PLAYS *Strife, The Eldest Son, The Skin Game, Justice, Loyalties*

Methuen's Theatre Classics

Methuen's Theatrescripts

If you would like to receive, free of charge, regular information about new plays and theatre books from Methuen, please send your name and address to:

The Marketing Department (Drama)
Methuen London Ltd
North Way
Andover
Hampshire SP10 5BE